STUDY GUIDE

crime scene
INVESTIGATION

Jacqueline T. *Fish*
Charleston Southern University

Larry S. *Miller*
East Tennessee State University

Michael C. *Braswell*
East Tennessee State University

Prepared by Dan Moeser

 LexisNexis®

 anderson publishing
A member of the LexisNexis Group

Crime Scene Investigation
STUDY GUIDE
Prepared by Dan Moeser

Copyright © 2007
Matthew Bender & Company, Inc., a member of the LexisNexis Group
Newark, NJ

Phone 877-374-2919
Web Site www.lexisnexis.com/anderson/criminaljustice

LexisNexis and the Knowledge Burst logo are trademarks of Reed Elsevier Properties, Inc.
Anderson Publishing is a registered trademark of Anderson Publishing Co., a member of the LexisNexis Group.

This Study Guide was designed to be used in conjunction with *Crime Scene Investigation*. © 2007 by Matthew Bender & Company, Inc. (ISBN: 978-1-59345-325-1)

Cover design by Tin Box Studio/Cincinnati, OH

EDITOR Ellen S. Boyne
ACQUISITIONS EDITOR Michael C. Braswell

Table of Contents

1 Introduction

In this opening chapter, you have been introduced to the world of crime scene investigation, the many aspects and expectations of this profession, and other specialized fields that overlap and contribute to the successful investigation. It is important for the aspiring crime scene investigator to realize this is a crucial position within the criminal justice system, but seldom provides the state-of-the-art facilities and equipment that are featured on today's television shows. Crime scene investigation remains the primary means of establishing linkages between a victim and a suspect or the suspect and the crime scene. The opportunities for success are increasing as scientific discoveries advance the application of technology to an ever-widening cross-disciplinary approach to solving crimes. Criminal justice programs across the nation are reporting larger numbers of students enrolling in undergraduate and graduate programs, which ensures a constant influx of new thoughts that lead to new discoveries.

As you continue through this textbook, you will be introduced to many new concepts and practices that will require you to develop insight into the processes that make crime scene investigation a valuable component of the criminal justice system. In order for you to apply the new knowledge you have gained from the textbook chapters and classroom lectures, you will be introduced to a crime scene investigation vignette titled "Holiday Homicide."

Learning Objectives

1. Describe the major goals of the crime scene search.
2. Define physical evidence.
3. Describe how physical evidence is located, handled, and stored.
4. Discuss the major factors that determine the value of physical evidence.
5. Describe what is meant by a "forensic scientist."
6. Define what an "expert witness" is and what purpose they serve.

7. Understand the ethical considerations that a CSI must consider while conducting an investigation.
8. Appreciate the "linkage" between location, suspect, and victim during a crime scene search.
9. Define "class" and "individual" characteristics of physical evidence.
10. Explain the legal considerations the CSI must follow and the reasons for those considerations.
11. Understand what "chain of custody" is and its importance.
12. Describe the ultimate goal of the CSI.

Key Terms

Chain of custody
Corpus delicti
Crime scene investigator (CSI)
Forensic anthropologist
Forensic nurse
Forensic scientist
Modus operandi (MO)
Physical evidence
Transient evidence

Chapter Outline

I.   Crime Scene Search

    A.   Recognition and identification of physical evidence

    B.   Collection and preservation of evidence

    C.   Reconstruction of the crime

    D.   Forming a theory about the crime

II. Crime Scene Investigator (CSI)

    A.   Interaction of the CSI and forensic scientist

    B.   Verifying jurisdiction

    C.   Determine if a crime has been committed

    D.   Providing proper evidence

    E.   Master skills in photography, sketching, and documentation of a crime

    F.   Reconstructing the crime scene

III.   Forensic Specialists

    A.   Archeologist

    B.   Botanist

    C.   Entomologist

    D.   Odontologist

    E.   Pathologist

    F.   Medical examiner

    G.   Coroner

IV.   Witnesses

    A.   Expert witnesses must be certified by the court. They should be articulate and have information that the average person would not have so they can educate the jury. They are legally and ethically bound to be truthful.

V.   Physical Evidence

    A.   Evidence that provides an accurate and objective crime scene search that tells the "story" of what happened. Physical evidence is used to provide impartial facts and is often referred to as the "silent witness."

VI.   Legal Issues

    A.   Search warrants

    B.   Standing operating procedures (SOPs)

    C.   Legislation (written laws)

    D.   Constitutional issues

    E.   Plain view

    F.   Fruit of the poisonous tree

    G.   Transient evidence

    H.   Supreme Court rulings

    I.   Chain of custody

True/False Questions

1.   Physical evidence is often referred to as the "silent witness."

2.   Forming a theory about a crime is NOT a major goal of a crime scene search.

3. Forensic science deals with the effective identification, documentation, collection, and preservation of physical evidence at the crime scene.

4. The testing procedures used to analyze the physical evidence in a case is NOT part of the CSI's responsibility.

5. A coroner is typically an elected or appointed official who conducts death investigations.

6. Reports by expert witnesses should be honest and written in technical terms.

7. The trial judge is responsible for determination of the qualifications of an expert witness under the Federal Rules of Evidence.

8. According to the text, the most critical aspect of a trial is that the guilty are convicted and the innocent are exonerated.

9. Linking a suspect to a victim is the most important and common type of linkage that can be established by physical evidence.

10. *Corpus delicti* means the preferred method of operation.

11. Physical evidence that can positively be linked to an individual is said to be class evidence.

12. The Fourth Amendment to the U.S. Constitution protects against unreasonable unreasonable search and seizures.

13. *Mincey v. Arizona* provides a court decision that dictates what actions law enforcement personnel are authorized to take without first obtaining a warrant.

14. Transient evidence is defined as physical evidence that may be lost forever if not immediately preserved.

15. The "*Frye* test" established the criteria that defines judicial acceptance of scientific advances.

16. "Chain of custody" refers to the linkage between physical evidence and its acceptance in court proceedings.

Multiple-Choice Questions

1. According to the text, what is *physical evidence* sometimes referred to as?
   a. all the facts of a case
   b. the silent witness
   c. behind the scene facts
   d. unspoken facts

2. Which is NOT a major goal of a crime scene search?
   a. recognition and identification on physical evidence
   b. collection and proper preservation of the evidence
   c. reconstruction of the crime
   d. presenting a formal announcement to the media as soon as possible

3. The four major factors that determine the value of physical evidence are:
   a. recognition, testing procedures, courtroom presentation, and collection
   b. collection, recognition, fingerprints, and courtroom presentation
   c. recognition, testing procedures, expert witnesses, and collection
   d. collection, expert witnesses, recognition, and testing procedures

4. According to the text, physical evidence leads to development of the linkage among:
   a. victim, witnesses, and perpetrator
   b. perpetrator, victim, and scene
   c. scene, witnesses, and victim
   d. latent prints, victim, and perpetrator

5. A death investigation is usually conducted by this elected official:
   a. medical examiner
   b. pathologist
   c. coroner
   d. lead investigator

6. According to the text, the essential elements of an expert witness's testimony are:
   a. clarity, completeness, and honesty
   b. honesty, clarity, and explainability
   c. understandability, simplicity, and honesty
   d. simplicity, honesty, and clarity

7. Under the Federal Rules of Evidence, who is responsible for determining the qualification of an expert witness?
    a. judge
    b. prosecutor
    c. defense counsel
    d. American Academy of Forensic Science

8. According to the text, what is considered the most critical aspect of a criminal trial?
    a. that, no matter what, the guilty person is convicted
    b. that the prosecutor presents adequate evidence to convict the suspect
    c. that the guilty are convicted and the innocent are exonerated
    d. that the innocent are never wrongfully convicted

9. According to the text, what is the most important and common type of linkage that can be established by physical evidence?
    a. linking a victim to a suspect
    b. linking a suspect to the crime scene
    c. linking a crime scene to the suspect
    d. linking a suspect to a victim

10. *Corpus delicti* means:
    a. preferred method of operation
    b. linkage between the victim, suspect, and location
    c. reconstruction of the crime scene
    d. providing essential information on the facts of the case

11. The *individual characteristics* of physical evidence are exemplified in:
    a. clothing and hair samples
    b. hair color and fingerprints
    c. fingerprints and DNA
    d. handwriting and bone structure

12. The _____ Amendment to the U.S. Constitution protects against unreasonable searches and seizures.
    a. Fifth
    b. Fourth
    c. Sixth
    d. Fourteenth

13. Transient evidence is defined as physical evidence that:
    a. may be lost forever if not immediately preserved
    b. is damaged or lost forever if not preserved properly
    c. is lost forever due to improper collection by the CSI
    d. may be lost forever if not recovered, collected, and transported immediately

14. Chain of custody usually refers to:
    a. documentation of all transient evidence
    b. documentation and location of all suspects
    c. documentation and location of all physical evidence
    d. documentation and location of crime scene photos, sketches, and notes

15. The "Frye test" refers to:
    a. acceptance of physical evidence in the federal court system
    b. acceptance of transient evidence in criminal trials
    c. acceptance of defense counsel's motion to dismiss the case
    d. established criteria that defines judicial acceptance of scientific advances

Discussion Questions

1. Discuss the basic principles for how a law enforcement officer should behave if he or she is the first officer on the scene. Specifically, what are the "Do's" and "Don'ts."

2. Discuss the general procedure of the crime scene investigator. What steps should be followed?

3. Discuss the importance of collecting evidence *legally*. Who determines the legality of the evidence? In the final analysis, who must be convinced of the importance of the evidence collected?

# The First Response

Patrol officers, firefighters, and emergency medical personnel are usually first to arrive on the scene, and generally all safety concerns will have been addressed before crime scene investigators enter the area. A CSI should assess the physical conditions of the location in order to identify hazards. In some instances, the level of personal protective equipment (PPE) that must be worn inside the crime scene may impact the amount of physical evidence that can be gathered as well as the amount of time a CSI can work within the secure perimeter. If the environment is toxic or potentially contaminated with chemical or biological hazards, a Hazmat Team will assume responsibility for developing the safety plan.

Before you enter a crime scene, be sure the location is within the legal boundaries of your jurisdiction. Do not overlook the need for a representative of the prosecutor's or solicitor's office to be notified of the situation. It is possible that search warrants must be secured before you can legally conduct a crime scene search.

Secure areas where the crime occurred and that are potential entry/exit paths of suspects and witnesses. When establishing boundaries, always secure a larger area and then reduce the area as additional information is determined that will decrease the perimeter of the scene. Isolation and protection are crucial to preserving transient evidence. In addition, multiple scenes may mean multiple jurisdictions are involved in the investigation. Most agencies will have multijurisdictional agreements that predetermine areas of responsibility in the event a crime expands into more than one jurisdiction.

Brief the detective taking charge of the scene upon completion of your responsibilities as a crime scene investigator. Relay all information and observations you have included in your notes. The CSI must always document factual information—not opinions.

Learning Objectives

1. Describe how to identify the scope of the crime scene.
2. Describe how a first responder would search a crime scene.
3. Explain what other officials may be on scene first and what their responsibilities are.
4. Describe the importance of proper jurisdiction over the crime scene.
5. Describe the safety concerns that need to be addressed at a crime scene.
6. Discuss the personal protection equipment (PPE) that may be required at the crime scene
7. Describe the specific factors that need to be considered when handling bloodborne pathogens.
8. Describe the initial walkthrough of the crime scene and what documentation should be collected.

Key Terms and Concepts

Biohazard bags
Biological fluids
Bloodborne pathogens
Coroner
Cross-contamination
Medical examiner
Personal protective equipment (PPE)
Preliminary walkthrough/assessment

Chapter Outline

I.   The First Responders and Their Duties/Responsibilities

    A.   Law enforcement personnel

    B.   Medical personnel

    C.   Firefighter personnel

II.   Potential Hazards at Crime Scenes

    A.   Chemical hazards

    B.   Biological hazards

    C.   Animals

    D.   Electrical/water hazards

    E.   Personal protective equipment required

III.   Control of Access/Egress of Crime Scene

    A.   Identify routes after discussion with CSI and lead detective.

    B.   Identify all personnel who enter restricted area.

    C.   Adhere to SOPs and ensure proper notification of supervisory personnel.

IV.   Canvassing the Crime Scene

    A.   Who should be interviewed?

    B.   Interviews should be done individually.

    C.   Proper identification must be requested.

    D.   Be alert for potential suspects.

True/False Questions

1.   Before initial entry of a crime scene, ensure that all safety concerns have been addressed.

2.   The crime scene investigator should enlist the assistance of medical and fire personnel to help clean up the scene.

3.   When securing a crime scene, potential entry/exit paths of suspects and witnesses should be included.

4.   Crime scene boundaries should start small and expand as more facts are received.

5.   The primary reason the CSI is dispatched to a crime scene is to ensure that all legal considerations have been met.

6.   The universal decontamination solution for body fluids is a 1:10 mixture of bleach or 70 percent isopropyl alcohol.

7.   One of the most common bloodborne pathogens is hepatitis.

8.   One of the most effective type of gloves to wear for protection are made of leather or fabric.

9.   According to the Hazardous Materials Identification System (HMIS), a blue warning label on a chemical container indicates a potential health hazard.

10.   The government agency that requires employers to provide Hazard Communication (HazCom) training is the Occupational Safety and Health Administration (OSHA).

11. One of the requirements of OSHA is to provide emergency and first aid procedures on chemical storage containers.

12. It is the responsibility of the senior medical person on the scene to take appropriate measures to safeguard individual health and ensure a safe working environment.

13. The initial walkthrough is to determine the nature and extent of the crime scene.

14. According to the text, crime scene searches should be conducted in an objective, systematic, and methodical manner.

15. Witnesses of a crime should be questioned together to get a consensus of what happened.

Multiple-Choice Questions

1. Usually, the first to arrive on the crime scene are:
   a. patrol officers
   b. firefighters
   c. emergency medical personnel
   d. all of the above

2. The CSI should document all emergency responders by obtaining, at a minimum:
   a. name, time of arrival, and agency
   b. name, badge number, and station assignment
   c. agency, station assignment, and time of arrival
   d. Documentation is not required.

3. When establishing boundaries of a crime scene, one should:
   a. secure a small controlled area first
   b. secure a large area and increase the perimeter as needed
   c. secure a large area and reduce as facts are determined
   d. secure entry and exit paths only

4. The primary reason the CSI is dispatched to a crime scene is to:
   a. identify all safety issues before allowing entry by personnel
   b. conduct an investigation
   c. document all personnel at the scene for possible questioning
   d. ensure that all legal considerations are met

5. The universal decontamination solution used to prevent cross-contamination is:
   a. diluted solution of bleach 1:10 or 70% isopropyl alcohol
   b. 70% isopropyl alcohol
   c. rubber gloves
   d. none of the above

6. The most common bloodborne pathogens are:
   a. human immunodeficiency virus, influenza, and common cold
   b. influenza, HIV-AIDS, and STDs
   c. HIV-AIDS, STDs, hepatitis, and influenza
   d. HIV-AIDS, rabies, hepatitis, and STDs

7. When using gloves, the following procedures should be followed:
   a. never wear leather or fabric gloves
   b. always use latex gloves
   c. never utilize the double-glove technique
   d. gloves of any type should be avoided

8. The government agency that sets safety standards for all workers is the:
   a. Occupational Safety and Hazard Administration
   b. Occupational Safety and Health Administration
   c. Occupational Hazard Materials Identification Administration
   d. Occupational Material Safety Administration

9. All chemicals must be properly labeled with the appropriate hazard warnings affixed to the containers. These labels are known as the:
   a. Hazardous Chemical Identification System
   b. Hazardous Material Safety System
   c. Hazardous Identification System
   d. Hazardous Materials Identification System

10. In the label system noted in Question 9, the label color that indicates a health hazard is:
    a. blue
    b. red
    c. yellow
    d. green

11. Information that must appear on a container includes:
    a. emergency procedures
    b. first-aid procedures
    c. name and contact information of manufacturer
    d. all of the above

12.   The initial walkthrough of a crime scene is to:
   a.   determine the nature and extent of the crime scene
   b.   identify all personnel at the scene
   c.   identify what additional personnel will be needed
   d.   none of the above

13.   According to the text, crime scene searches must be conducted:
   a.   immediately, completely, and methodically
   b.   methodically, in accordance with written procedures, and immediately
   c.   immediately, systematically, and objectively
   d.   systematically, objectively, and methodically

14.   When the scene includes the death of a person, it must be processed as if:
   a.   a homicide has occurred
   b.   a natural death has occurred until proven otherwise
   c.   no crime was committed unless proven otherwise
   d.   none of the above

15.   When witnesses are located at the crime scene:
   a.   keep all witnesses together
   b.   keep all witnesses separate
   c.   ask witnesses to provide a written statement of what they saw
   d.   tell witnesses they will be contacted if needed at a later time

Discussion Questions

1.   Discuss the "big picture" that a first responder should keep in mind when arriving on scene.

2.   Who should and shouldn't be allowed to enter a crime scene, and what procedures should be used for authorized responders?

3.   While no two crime scenes are exactly alike, discuss the general procedures for the initial assessment of a crime scene.

3 Documenting the Crime Scene

The primary goal of a crime scene investigation is to reconstruct what happened and identify the perpetrators of the crime. To this end, the CSI should conduct an investigation that will help determine the sequence of events, the identity and movements of victims and perpetrators, and the location of evidence. Each item of evidence must be collected, identified, and documented. Remember that as these steps take place, it is possible to uncover additional evidence. Follow the same procedure to first document, and then collect the new evidence. Each item must be closed, sealed, marked, and identified on the evidence log when collected.

Establish and maintain the chain of custody. When the evidence sample is collected, it must be sealed and marked by the CSI. Time, date, location, and the CSI's name or initials must be on the outside of each seal. Individual department policies may dictate additional information, such as an incident or case number.

Obtain control or standard samples in addition to the evidentiary physical evidence. It is important for the CSI to recognize that the crime laboratory will need standard samples for comparison purposes. Soil, vegetation, and insects may be vital as comparison standards for establishing the location and age of evidence. If the evidence is not identifiable, it will be analyzed and compared to reference libraries containing reference samples in an effort to determine the origin of the evidence. Consider the need to obtain elimination samples from others who had access to the crime scene. It may be necessary to obtain search warrants prior to obtaining these samples, and this determination should be left up to the detective working the case.

Crime scene notes, photographs, and the sketch will provide the best documentation of the crime scene investigation. None of the techniques can be used alone, and you should record everything that has been done in an investigation.

Do not give up control of the scene until you are certain you have conducted a complete and thorough search. In the case of a homicide investigation or suspicious death, it may be necessary to retain control of the scene until after the autopsy is complete or preliminary forensic testing is complete.

Learning Objectives

1. Describe the main objective of a crime scene investigation.
2. List the tools that are required to document the crime scene properly.
3. Describe what *transient evidence* is and why it is different than other types of evidence.
4. Describe the process of taking photographs: Where do you start? What do you take photos of? Why do you take photos?
5. What is meant by "painting with light"?
6. Explain how to determine what film type and speed to use.
7. List the three types of cameras and what their differences are.
8. Describe what a *sketch* of a crime scene is and why it is important.
9. Know what the types of sketches are and the differences between them.
10. List the four methods for taking measurements and locating evidence at a crime scene.
11. Explain the circumstances under which each measurement method would be used.
12. Understand the legality of searching a crime scene, especially when it is located on private property.
13. Describe the four exceptions that allow for a search of a crime scene without prior permission.
14. List the proper order for collection and preservation of evidence.
15. Explain basically how a search should be conducted
16. List and explain the six types of search patterns and when each would be used.
17. Describe the unique problems associated with searching a vehicle, and list the most likely areas in which to find latent fingerprints.

Key Terms and Concepts

ASA/ISO
Baseline measures
Dedicated flash
Grid search
Legend
Link search
Painting with light
Perspective grid
Pixelated image
Polar coordinates
Spiral search
Strip search
Transient evidence
Triangulation
Wheel search
Zone search

Chapter Outline

I.   Main Objectives of a Crime Scene Investigation

    A.   Reconstruct the incident

    B.   Ascertain the sequence of events

    C.   Determine the method of operation (*modus operandi*)

    D.   Disclose the motive

    E.   Uncover what property was stolen and from where

    F.   Determine what the criminal may have done before, during, and after the event

    G.   Identify, recover, and preserve physical evidence of the crime

II.   Photography

    A.   Why photography is used

    B.   How and why photography is documented

    C.   What items should be photographed?

    D.   Painting with light

    E.   Types of cameras

    F.   Types of film to use

    G.   Camera lenses and filters

III. Sketches

    A.   Types of sketches

    B.   Reason for sketches

    C.   How sketches should be drawn

IV. Measurements

    A.   Types of methods for taking measurements
       1.   Triangulation
       2.   Baseline
       3.   Polar coordinates
       4.   Perspective grid

    B.   When each method is used

V. Searching the Scene

    A.   Legal considerations
       1.   When a warrant is required
       2.   When a warrant is not required
          a.   Emergency
          b.   To prevent destruction of evidence
          c.   Consent
          d.   Lawful arrest

    B.   Agency Standard Operating Procedures (SOPs)

    C.   Weather considerations

    D.   Communication between all investigators

    E.   Chain-of-custody requirements

    F.   Order of collection of evidence
       1.   Transient
       2.   Biological
       3.   Latent

    G.   Order of a systematic search
       1.   Most to least transient evidence
       2.   Least to most intrusive process methods

    H.   Vehicle searches
       1.   Legal considerations
       2.   Searching before moving; searching after moving
       3.   Locating latent prints

True/False Questions

1. The main purpose of documentation is to record and preserve the location and relationship of physical evidence at the crime scene

2. Determining the *modus operandi* is one of the main objectives of a crime scene investigation.

3. *Transient evidence* refers to physical evidence that must be transported with special considerations.

4. The three ways to document evidence at a crime scene are photography, sketches, and notes.

5. When photographing a crime scene, the normal procedure is to start at the center and work away from the scene to include entrances/exits to the scene.

6. When photographing a crime scene, a high-speed film of ASA/ISO 400 or higher should be used.

7. Higher-speed films are useful for low-light situations but are not as sharp and clear as lower-speed films.

8. Digital cameras should be used when there is a need for enlargements of 11 x 14 inches or more.

9. A crime scene sketch is the permanent record of the actual size and distance relationships of the scene and physical evidence.

10. The three types of sketches that can be drawn to depict the crime scene are the overhead view, the rough sketch, and the final sketch.

11. Triangulation measurements are generally made for outdoor scenes in which there are no right angles.

12. Baseline measures are the most common form of crime scene measurement and are generally used for indoor crime scenes.

13. Polar coordinates is a method of taking measurements and is a three-dimensional coordinate system used to indicate a location of an item.

14. Perspective-grid measures do not require 90-degree angles and can be used for outdoor or indoor crime scenes.

15. The Fourth Amendment to the U.S. Constitution protects against unreasonable searches and seizures of property.

16. The proper order for collection and preservation of evidence is: transient, biological, then latent.

Multiple-Choice Questions

1. The main purpose of documentation of a crime scene is to:
   a. reconstruct the crime scene, identify a suspect, and assist the prosecutor
   b. record and preserve the location and relationship of physical evidence
   c. obtain a motive for the crime, determine *modus operandi*, and identify a suspect
   d. none of the above

2. According to the text, the three ways to document evidence at a crime scene are:
   a. digital pictures, notes, and sketches
   b. sketches, photo log, and notes
   c. photography, notes, and sketches
   d. overhead view, video, and notes

3. Examples of *transient evidence* are:
   a. hairs, fibers, and wet shoeprints
   b. latent fingerprints, clothing, and weapons
   c. blood, semen, and fibers
   d. none of the above

4. According to the text, when using photography at a crime scene, the film speed should be at least:
   a. ASA/ISO 100 or higher
   b. ASA/ISO 200 or higher
   c. ASA/ISO 300 or higher
   d. ASA/ISO 400 or higher

5. Polarizing filters are used when photographing:
   a. very small objects
   b. shiny surfaces
   c. very large objects
   d. none of the above

6. A crime scene sketch is the permanent record of:
   a. size and distance relationships of the scene and physical evidence
   b. a hand-drawn picture of who was present at the scene
   c. where furniture and pictures were located at the scene
   d. eyewitnesses account of the crime

7. The three types of sketches that can be drawn to depict the crime scene are:
   a. eye-level, overhead view, and elevation view
   b. elevation view, 3D view, and baseline view
   c. 3D view, baseline view, and elevation view
   d. overhead view, elevation view, and 3D view

8. The four methods for taking measurements and locating evidence at the crime scene are:
   a. Perspective grid, polar coordinates, baseline, and triangulation
   b. Triangulation, polar coordinates, overhead, and baseline
   c. Baseline, overhead, triangulation, and perspective grid
   d. polar coordinates, baseline, triangulation, and perspective grid

9. The most common form of indoor measurement is the:
   a. perspective grid
   b. triangulation
   c. baseline
   d. overhead

10. Baseline measurements require:
    a. 45-degree angles
    b. acute angles
    c. right angles
    d. oblique angles

11. Which measurement requires the use of a transit or compass to measure the angles?
    a. perspective grid
    b. triangulation
    c. overhead
    d. polar coordinates

12. Which measurement system is also known as photogrammetry?
    a. polar coordinates
    b. triangulation
    c. perspective grid
    d. overhead

13. Which Constitutional Amendment protects against unreasonable searches and seizures?
    a.   First
    b.   Fourth
    c.   Fifth
    d.   Sixth

14. The proper order for collection and preservation of evidence is:
    a.   transient, biological, then latent
    b.   biological, physical, then latent
    c.   latent, transient, then physical
    d.   none of the above

Discussion Questions

1. Discuss the importance of documenting a crime scene. What are the objectives, and what is the importance of each?

2. Discuss the tools needed to document a crime scene properly. What is the importance of each?

3. When prioritizing the search procedures of a crime scene, what is the usual order for collection and preservation of evidence, and what is the importance of each?

4 Fingerprints and Palmprints

There are more than 47 million sets of fingerprints maintained in the FBI's criminal file, which is the largest database in the world. Responses can be generated within two hours if the fingerprints are submitted electronically to the IAFIS, which has been operational since 1999. Again, while the search and comparison can be automated, a human must still verify the match between the two prints and be qualified to testify in court regarding the veracity of the identification.

Learning Objectives

1. Describe what a fingerprint or palmprint is.
2. List the different classes of fingerprints, and describe each.
3. Explain what comprises the residue of fingerprints or palmprints.
4. List and describe the four types of fingerprints
5. Explain the procedure for obtaining inked fingerprints/palmprints.
6. What is meant by *elimination prints*?
7. Understand the unique process for obtaining fingerprints from the deceased.
8. Explain when fingerprints are formed and the differences between the fingerprints of a child and those of an adult.
9. Describe what a *latent* fingerprint is.
10. Understand what will normally constitute a legal print in a court of law.
11. Describe the ways to locate latent prints.
12. Describe the ways to lift and document latent prints.
13. Describe the advantages and shortcoming of each lifting process.
14. Understand the AFIS.

Key Terms and Concepts

AFIS (Automated Fingerprint Identification System)
Arches
Alternate light source (ALS)
CBC
Daubert rulings
DFO
Gentian violet
IND
Inked impressions
Loops
Minutia
Ninhydrin
Plain impressions
Small particle reagent (SPR)
Whorls

Chapter Outline

I.   Fingerprint Classes

    A.   Loops (65%)
        1.   Ulna (toward little finger)
        2.   Radial (toward thumb)

    B.   Whorls (30%)
        1.   Plain
        2.   Central
        3.   Pocket loop
        4.   Double loop
        5.   Accidental

    C.   Arches (5%)
        1.   Plain
        2.   Tented

    D.   Cores and deltas

II.   Principles of Fingerprints and Palmprints

    A.   What are ridges and grooves, and where are they?

    B   What are fingerprints made of?

    C.   When are palmprints used?

III.   Using Fingerprints as Evidence

    A.   Four types of fingerprints
        1.   Visible
        2.   Plastic
        3.   Latent
        4.   Wet

    B.   Preserving fingerprints as evidence

IV.   Inked Impressions

    A.   Fingerprint card

    B.   Rolling prints

    C.   Reasons for fingerprint card being rejected

    D.   Reasons for plain or flat impressions on fingerprint card

V.   Elimination Prints

VI.   Suspect Prints

VII.   Fingerprinting the Deceased

    A.   Uniqueness compared to living person

    B.   Processes used to obtain fingerprint

    C.   Superglue fuming

VIII.   Establishing Identity

    A.   Twins

    B.   When prints are formed

IX.   Latent Fingerprints

    A.   Consists of oils and/or perspiration on a surface, usually invisible

    B.   Differences between adults' and children's prints

    C.   Method of processing depends on type and location of surface and physical conditions of crime scene
        1,   Powder (dusting)
        2.   DFO
        3.   Ninhydrin
        4.   Physical developer
        5.   Portable fuming wands (Superglue)
        6.   Iodine crystals (Superglue)
        7.   SPR (small particle reagent)—used for wet or greasy items with latent prints

D.   Preserving for evidence. Always photograph first.

E.   Determining how many *friction ridge characters* must be obtained for a valid positive ID

F.   Most common way to locate latent fingerprints at a crime scene

X.   Automated Fingerprint Identification System (AFIS)

True/False Questions

1.   Fingerprints are a reproduction of friction skin ridges found on the palm side of the fingers.

2.   The layer of skin on which we find fingerprints is the epidermis layer.

3.   The main ingredients of a fingerprint are perspiration and oils.

4.   Fingerprint residue is comprised of only organic substances secreted from the eccrine (sweat) glands.

5.   Palmprints are maintained in an extensive database similar to fingerprints.

6.   The four types of fingerprints are: visible, plastic, latent, and wet.

7.   Fingerprints should not be photographed until all steps in the preserving process have been completed.

8.   The number one reason for fingerprint cards to be rejected by the IAFIS is the failure of the fingerprint technician to fully roll the "bulb" of each finger from nail to nail and the tip to the first joint.

9.   The main advantage of taking fingerprints using a digital-based biometric system is that the prints can be immediately sent for classification and matching.

10.   *Plain* impressions are used to verify that all fingers have been printed.

11.   When taking fingerprints of a deceased person, the use of a "dead man's spoon" is often used.

12.   Identical twins are the only people who will have the same fingerprints.

13.   Latent fingerprints are generally invisible to the naked eye.

14. Latent fingerprints of adults and children will survive for days and sometimes even weeks.

15. Latent fingerprints are not affected by heat and cold temperatures as long as the proper amount of powder is used.

16. Some of the more common chemical processes used to lift latent fingerprints are silver nitrate, iodine fuming, and ninhydrin.

17. The International Association for Identification has concluded that there must be at least eight friction ridge characteristics identified before the impression can be said to have positive identification.

18. The most common method of locating latent fingerprints at a crime scene is the use of a high-power light source.

19. The chemical that is used for wet latent prints is small particle reagent (SPR).

20. Ninhydrin is most effective when processing nonporous surfaces.

21. The standard technique for preserving latent prints is to place clear adhesive fingerprint tape over the print and then place the tape on a contrasting cardboard background.

22. According to the text, the process that has been found to be the most effective means of processing a body for latent fingerprints is "Superglue fuming."

23. According to the text, the most important function of the Automated Fingerprint Identification System (AFIS) is if a fingerprint is a "match," there is no further examination required.

24. According to the text, there are approximately 470 million sets of fingerprints maintained in the FBI's criminal file.

Multiple-Choice Questions

1. All fingerprints are divided into three classes of general patterns:
    a. loops, deltas, betas
    b. radial, loops, arches
    c. whorls, loops, arches
    d. arches, deltas, loops

2. The fingerprint pattern that is most common is the:
    a.   loop
    b.   arch
    c.   whorl
    d.   none of the above

3. Fingerprints are mostly comprised of:
    a.   oils
    b.   organic substances
    c.   water
    d.   inorganic substances

4. Which of the following statements is true about palmprints?
    a.   Since the discovery of DNA, palmprints are never used for identi-fication.
    b.   Palmprints are often used for identification; however, there is not an extensive database for maintenance of the files.
    c.   Palmprints are gathered when processing individuals arrested for routine criminal charges and are maintained in the extensive data-base by the FBI.
    d.   Palmprints are often used for identification and are maintained in an extensive database

5. The four types of fingerprints are:
    a.   visible, dry, latent, and plastic
    b.   latent, inked, plastic, and wet
    c.   wet, plastic, molded, and latent
    d.   latent, plastic, wet, and visible

6. The main reason for fingerprint cards to be rejected is:
    a.   failure to fully roll the "bulb" of each finger
    b.   failure to fully photograph the fingerprint
    c.   failure to take fingerprints in the proper sequence
    d.   failure to properly identify the person being fingerprinted

7. *Plain or flat* impressions are used to:
    a.   verify the ridges of the rolled fingerprint
    b.   verify the grooves of the rolled fingerprint
    c.   verify the proper sequence of the fingerprints
    d.   none of the above

8. Which statement is NOT associated with the use of a *dead man's spoon:*
   a. A dead man's spoon is used when taking "inked" fingerprints.
   b. A dead man's spoon is used for lifting latent fingerprints.
   c. A dead man's spoon is used with a fingerprint card that has been cut into strips.
   d. A dead man's spoon is used when obtaining "rolled" fingerprint impressions.

9. Which statement is true concerning fingerprints?
   a. All individuals except identical twins have different fingerprints.
   b. All individuals have different fingerprints.
   c. All individuals except fraternal twins have different fingerprints.
   d. none of the above

10. Latent fingerprints are created by the deposit of:
    a. oils and/or perspiration
    b. perspiration and water
    c. water and organic substances
    d. water and inorganic substances

11. Research has shown that latent fingerprints left by an adult may survive for:
    a. months or even years
    b. less time than for a child
    c. an extended time if kept in extreme-heat conditions
    d. days and even weeks

12. After making a latent print visible, the next procedure should be:
    a. preserving the print with fingerprint tape
    b. photographing the print
    c. removing all excess powder to avoid smearing
    d. spraying the print with lacquer to help preserve it

13. According to the text, the minimum number of friction ridge character-istics that must be present in two impressions in order to establish posi-tive identification in a court of law are:
    a. eight
    b. 10
    c. There is no predetermined number.
    d. 12

14. The proper sequence for "lifting" a latent print is:
    a.   apply fingerprint powder, photograph, apply fingerprint tape, then apply tape to contrasting card
    b.   photograph print, spray print with clear lacquer, apply fingerprint tape, then apply tape to contrasting card
    c.   apply fingerprint powder, spray print with clear lacquer, apply fingerprint tape, then apply tape to contrasting card
    d.   apply fingerprint powder, spray print with clear lacquer, photograph, apply fingerprint tape, then apply tape to contrasting card

15. What works like a liquid fingerprint powder and is used on wet or greasy items?
    a.   DFO (1,8-diazafluoren-9-one)
    b.   small particle reagent (SPR)
    c.   Superglue fuming
    d.   silver nitrate

16. This system converts the images of a fingerprint into digital minutiae and records the relative position and orientation of the minutiae:
    a.   the Automated Fingerprint Identification System (AFIS)
    b.   the Automated Fingerprint System (AFS)
    c.   the Automated Latent Fingerprint System (ALFS)
    d.   none of the above

Discussion Questions

1.   Discuss the classes of general patterns of fingerprints. What are their differences, and how do they relate to the general population?

2.   Discuss the different types of fingerprints. What are the challenges of each? What are the different procedures used for each, especially if they are to be used in a court of law.

3.   Discuss the method(s) used to locate fingerprints. What are the different procedures used for each method? If more than one method can be used, which method should be tried first? Why?

5 Trace and Impression Evidence

Edmond Locard is credited with recognizing the theory of exchange. He stated very accurately that every contact leaves a trace. Also referred to as *Locard's Theory of Exchange*, this concept basically supports the following three statements:

1. Traces of the victim and the scene will be carried away by the perpetrator.

2. Traces of the perpetrator will remain on the victim, and the victim may leave traces of himself or herself on the perpetrator.

3. Traces of the perpetrator will be left at the scene.

Any item *can* and *may* be physical evidence that a crime has occurred. Trace evidence can provide valuable leads for investigators, but it first must be recognized as evidence by the CSI. Even if the trace evidence cannot be positively identified as having originated from a sole source to the exclusion of all others, trace evidence can corroborate other types of evidence and link the suspect to the crime, to the victim, or to a specific item.

Learning Objectives

1. Explain Locard's *Theory of Transfer*.
2. Describe what *trace evidence* is.
3. Explain why the crime scene investigator should collect *comparison samples*.
4. Explain where hairs may come from, what they may reveal, and how they are collected.

5. Explain where fibers may come from, what they may reveal, and how they are collected.
6. Describe how glass fragments can help in an investigation and what cracks in window glass may reveal.
7. Describe what the soil at a crime may reveal.
8. Describe what gunshot residue may reveal to an investigator.
9. Explain how residue may be left on an offender, victim, or witness and how the investigator can obtain the trace evidence.
10. Understand what *impression evidence* is, how it is located, and how to preserve the evidence.
11. Explain the difference between bitemarks made on a living person compared to bitemarks made on a dead person.
12. List the four findings that can be related to the examination of bitemarks by a forensic odontologist.
13. Explain the technique used to locate footwear or other impressions at indoor crime scenes.
14. Explain the technique used to obtain an impression of footwear.
15. Explain the technique used to obtain an impression in the snow.

Key Terms and Concepts

ABFO scale
Control or blank sample
Dental stone
Electrostatic dust print lifter
Elimination samples
Impression evidence
Locard's Theory of Exchange
Standard or reference sample

Chapter Outline

I.   Locard's Theory of Exchange

   A.   Traces of the victim and the scene will be carried away by the perpetrator.

   B.   Traces of the perpetrator will remain on the victim, and the victim may leave traces of himself or herself on the perpetrator.

   C.   Traces of the perpetrator will be left at the scene.

II. Hairs

    A.   Human or animal

    B.   Unique properties

    C.   Mitochondrial DNA analysis

    D.   Reveal race, drug use, and color of hair

    E.   50 hair samples from head and 24 from pubic area are needed for comparison

III. Fibers

    A.   Manmade

    B.   Natural from animals

    C.   Natural from plants

    D.   Preserve fiber evidence by inserting sheets of paper between layers

IV. Glass

    A.   Glass fragments typically yield only class characteristics

    B.   Glass fragments found on victim

    C.   Fracture patterns
        1.   Radial
        2.   Concentric

    D.   FBI database for density and refractive indices and elemental analyses

V. Soil

    A.   Always collect soil, even if a definite crime scene has not been determined

    B.   Soil is always darker when wet

    C.   There are more than 1,100 different colors of soil

    D.   Never dislodge soil from shoes or garments

    E.   Always collect control samples

VI. Gunshot Residue

    A.   Primer, lead, barium, and antimony are deposited on shooter's hand

    B.   Use cotton swab moistened with nitric acid and wipe hands

    C.   Residue can last up to six hours after weapon has been fired

    D.   Deceased victim's hands should be covered with paper bags before transport to protect potential evidence

VII. Impression Evidence

    A.   Footwear
          1.   May reveal shoe size, unique tread patterns, and number of suspects
          2.   Impressions can be damaged by weather, people, vehicles
          3.   Two forms of footwear evidence—impressions and prints
              a.   Impressions: Photograph first, then cast. Two sets of photos—with and without a scale. Or use oblique lighting then photograph.
              b.   Prints: If footwear is located, ink bottoms, put footwear on feet, and step on white paper or Mylar. Use same procedure for bare feet.

    B.   Tire Impressions
          1.   FBI maintains a tire tread database to determine manufacturer
          2.   Cast using dental stone
          3.   Scrape name, date, and case number on back of cast and let dry.

VIII. Bitemarks

    A.   Tooth pattern

    B.   Possible DNA from saliva

    C.   Differences of bitemarks: antemortem (less distinctive) and postmortem (well-defined indentions but no bruising).

    D.   Photographs are mandatory, with and without an ABFO scale.

    E.   Forensic odontologist will usually have one of four conclusions
          1.   Definite—to the exclusion of all others
          2.   Consistent—no features present that will exclude the suspect
          3.   Possible—due to nature of injury, unable to positively confirm or exclude the suspect
          4.   Exclusionary—definitely not made by the suspect.

True/False Questions

1. A comparison sample is also called a control sample.

2. Human hairs can reveal an individual's race.

3. Human hairs can reveal an individual's age.

4. Human hairs can reveal an individual's hair color.

5. When gathering control samples, 50 full lengths of hair should be taken from the head and 24 hairs from the pubic region.

6. At the present time, it is not possible to distinguish between human and animal hair.

7. The most prevalent plant fiber is cotton.

8. The two broad groups of fibers are plant and manmade.

9. Scientific analysis can positively match a fiber strand to a garment.

10. The proper way to package fiber evidence is to insert sheets of paper between the layers of clothing and on top of clothing to avoid cross-contamination.

11. The two kinds of physical evidence are *class* evidence and *individual* evidence.

12. Glass fragment examination generally yields only class characteristics, not individual characteristics.

13. The two types of fractures that occur on a window glass are *radial* and *concentric*.

14. The ATF maintains a database that contains the density and refractive indices and elemental analyses of glass.

15. Soil is usually darker in color when wet.

16. Scientists estimate that there are more than 1,100 different soil colors.

17. When a gun is fired, gases and powder create what is called *blowback*.

18. Gunshot residue may remain on a subject's hand for up to 12 hours after a weapon has been fired.

19. Footwear impressions are useful to tell the size of the shoe and tread patterns.

20. There are two forms of footwear evidence—*impressions* and *prints*.

21. The U.S. Customs Service maintains a tire tread database that crime lab examiners can access for comparison purposes.

22. Bitemarks made on a living victim are less distinctive than those made on a deceased person.

23. The four findings that can be related to the examination of bitemarks, provided a suspect has been identified, are: definite, consistent, possible, and exclusionary.

24. According to the text, dental stone is most commonly used for casting fingerprints.

25. According to the text, to enhance the visibility of impressions in snow, you should lightly spray gray primer paint into the impressions.

Multiple-Choice Questions

1. Which statement is NOT part of Locard's Theory of Transfer:
   a. Traces of the victim and the scene will be carried away by the perpetrator.
   b. Traces of only the victim will be found at the scene.
   c. Traces of the perpetrator will be left at the scene.
   d. Traces of the perpetrator will remain on the victim, and the victim may leave traces of himself or herself on the perpetrator.

2. In addition to collecting a comparison sample, what addition samples should be collected?
   a. unique
   b. physical
   c. control
   d. microscopic

3. According to the text, human hairs can reveal:
   a. color of hair
   b. blood type
   c. age
   d. none of the above

4. When gathering control samples for the laboratory, how many hairs should you collect from the head and pubic area?
   a. 40 head and 25 pubic
   b. 50 head and 30 pubic
   c. 60 head and 24 pubic
   d. 50 head and 24 pubic

5. The most prevalent plant fiber is:
    a.   cotton
    b.   rayon
    c.   wildflower
    d.   honeysuckle

6. The two broad groups of fibers are:
    a.   cotton and wildflower
    b.   manmade and natural
    c.   synthetic and cotton
    d.   none of the above

7. Generally, glass fragment examination yields what kind of characteristics?
    a.   general
    b.   class
    c.   individual
    d.   unique

8. Determining the direction and force of an impact on window glass can be accomplished by examining the _____ surrounding the hole.
    a.   diameter
    b.   thickness of the glass
    c.   fracture patterns
    d.   extent of breakage

9. A pattern that encircles the hole or point of impact would be a _____ pattern.
    a.   concentric
    b.   radial
    c.   whorl
    d.   unique

10. The agency that maintains a database that contains the density and refractive indices and elemental analyses for glass is the:
    a.   ATF
    b.   FBI
    c.   Customs Service
    d.   Bureau of Glass Investigations

11. Scientists estimate there are _____ different soil colors.
    a.   more than 3,000
    b.   about 800
    c.   about 1,200
    d.   more than 1,100

12. Blowback on the rear of the gun when fired is caused by:
    a. primer and lead
    b. gases and powder
    c. powder and primer
    d. gases and primer

13. To protect all trace evidence, deceased victims should have their hands:
    a. bagged
    b. photographed
    c. wrapped in plastic
    d. tied together

14. According to the text, before using forceps to recover items such as hairs or fibers, be sure to clean the forceps with:
    a. warm soapy water
    b. cold water and no soap
    c. bleach and water solution
    d. a cotton swab with alcohol solution

15. The two forms of footwear evidence are impressions and:
    a. marks
    b. outlines
    c. ridges
    d. prints

16. A tire tread database is maintained by:
    a. the FBI
    b. the ATF
    c. the Customs Service
    d. tire manufacturing companies

17. Bitemarks are less distinctive on a _____ person than those on a _____ person.
    a. deceased; living
    b. living; injured
    c. antemortem; deceased
    d. none of the above

18. Provided a suspect has been identified, the four findings that can be related to the examination of bitemarks are:
    a. exclusionary, possible, match, definite
    b. possible, consistent, exclusionary, definite
    c. definite, consistent, possible, unmatched
    d. possible, definite, exclusionary, likely

19. According to the text, tire impressions should be cast using _____ to preserve the impression and create a three-dimensional model of the tire tracks.
    a. dental stone
    b. Quickcrete
    c. plastic resin
    d. dental glue

20. According to the text, to highlight the ridges and grooves of impressions in snow, one should:
    a. spray clear lacquer over the ridges and grooves
    b. spray black paint over the ridges and grooves
    c. spray gray primer paint over the ridges and grooves
    d. spray white paint over the ridges and grooves

Discussion Questions

1. What is *trace evidence*? List examples. Explain the general procedures for collecting this evidence.

2. Generally, why is preserving trace evidence important? What pitfalls should be avoided?

3. List several potential areas of trace evidence and the procedures for collecting and preserving each.

6 Body Fluid Evidence

Forensic biology is the study of life and includes both cellular and microbiology subspecialities. The analysis of the properties and effects of serums (blood, semen, saliva, sweat, or fecal matter) is called serology and is an essential step in the examination of physical evidence. These analyses cross multiple disciplines and include biology, chemistry, immunology, and genetics. At the crime scene, the most frequently encountered biological stains are blood, seminal fluid, and saliva; however, others—including vaginal secretions, urine, and feces—may also be discovered.

Learning Objectives

1. Define forensic niology.
2. List the many serums of serology.
3. Understand what toxicology is and what its purpose is.
4. Understand what DNA is and what purpose it serves.
5. Describe what the CODIS system is and who maintains it.
6. Describe what presumptive blood tests are used for.
7. Understand the make-up of seminal fluid, the substance found only in semen, and the proof positive test performed for the detection of PSA.
8. Describe the procedure the crime scene investigator uses to located, collect, and preserve body fluid evidence.
9. Explain what a physical evidence recovery kit is.
10. Describe how clothing should be handled when potential evidence may be obtained.
11. Understand the use of luminol and fluorescein and what items can cause false positive readings.

Key Terms

CODIS (Combined DNA Index System)
Confirmatory test
EDTA
Forensic biology
Gas chromatography
Mass spectrometry
Mitochondrial DNA (mtDNA)
Presumptive tests
Prostate-specific antigen (PSA)
Serology
Sexual assault nurse examiner (SANE)
Touch DNA
Toxicology

Chapter Outline

I.   Forensic niology is the study of life and includes cellular and microbiology subspecialties.

II.   Toxicology

    A.   Study of body fluids, tissues, and organs for presence of drugs or poisons

    B   Presumptive tests

    C.   Confirmatory tests—(CG/MS)

III. DNA

    A.   Sir Alec Jeffreys

    B.   All individuals different except identical twins

    C.   Where we carry DNA (blood, saliva, seminal fluid)

    D.   What is DNA
        1.   Organic compound
        2.   Found in chromosomes of nuclei of cells
        3.   Mitochondrial DNA (mtDNA) from mother only
        4.   CODIS
           a.   Maintained by FBI
           b.   Convicted felons
        5.   Stability of DNA

6. Touch DNA
    a. Anything that a perpetrator has handled
    b. A latent print is part perspiration (DNA)
    c. Fingerprint powders/chemical processing agents do not interfere with the collection of epithelial cells

IV. Blood

    A. Presumptive tests

    B. Confirmatory tests

V. Seminal Fluid

    A. Composition of semen
    1. 95% seminal fluid
    2. 5% spermatozoa

    B. Male ejaculation
    1. Less than a teaspoon
    2. 200 million spermatozoa

    C. Use of UV light to locate seminal fluid
    1. Prostate-specific antigen (PSA) only found in semen
    2. PSA increases with age

    D. Collection
    1. Sterile swab or gauze
    2. Apply reagent
    3. Purple color shows good indication of semen

VI. Other Body Fluids

    A. Saliva
    1. Cigarette butts, beer/soda cans, bottles, glass, bites
    2. Best potential DNA from first urination of the day

VII. Locating, Collecting, and Preserving Body Fluid Evidence

    A. Sterile cotton swabs or gauze patches
    1. Saturate swab
    2. Air dry
    3. Control swab

    B. Physical evidence recovery kits (PERKs)

    C. Preserving clothing as evidence
    1. Photograph all clothing first
    2. Air-dry all clothing with paper underneath before packaging
    3. Use paper to wrap. Put paper between each piece.

D.   Locating
    1.   UV light
    2.   ALS or laser
    3.   Most body fluids fluoresce. Blood absorbs light and appears black
    4.   Use of luminol and fluorescein
        a.   Neither will interfere with DBA tests
        b.   False positives

True/False Questions

1.   The most frequently encountered biological stains found at a crime scene are blood, seminal fluid and saliva.

2.   Toxicology is concerned with confirming the presence of drugs or poisons.

3.   A *confirmatory test* is done by the CSI at the crime scene.

4.   The instrument most commonly used to detect any organic chemical in body fluids, tissues or organs is the gas chromatography-mass spectrometry (GC/MS).

5.   Urine tests provide a timeline that indicates drug use over a long period of time.

6.   While wet body fluids can carry diseases, body fluids that have dried do not.

7.   Sir Alec Jeffreys discovered the first *deoxyribonucleic acid* (DNA) "fingerprints."

8.   For a DNA to be obtained from seminal fluid, there must be sperm present.

9.   Identical twins have the exact same genetic makeup.

10.   Mitochondrial DNA is transmitted by the father only.

11.   The FBI established and maintains the Combined DNA Index System (CODIS).

12.   CODIS contains profiles of all individuals incarcerated since 1998.

13.   DNA can remain intact for years.

14. DNA analysis can be done on latent prints but must be completed before any chemical processing agents have been used.

15. One of the presumptive tests for detecting blood is the MacPhail's Reagent Test.

16. Presumptive tests are tests done at the crime lab to confirm a field test done by the CSI.

17. Semen is composed of approximately 95 percent seminal fluid and 5 percent spermatozoa.

18. Prostate specific antigen (PSA) is a substance that is present in semen and is not found in any other body fluid.

19. An IR light causes seminal stains to fluoresce.

20. Detection of PSA is positive proof of the presence of semen.

21. According to the text, rape is a sexually motivated crime, and seminal evidence is almost always present.

22. Sperm heads have been detected in deceased persons for up to seven days after intercourse in the vaginal cavity.

23. Urine stains are primarily composed of water and salts and are not usually successful in DNA analysis.

24. Research has shown that the first urination of the day provides the best sample for generating a DNA profile.

25. When using an alternate light source or forensic light source on blood, the blood will appear black in color.

26. Luminol is a chemiluminescent compound used to determine the presence of blood in the absence of visual stains.

27. Fluorescein is used to detect blood stains that are not visible and is not affected by household bleach.

28. According to the text, all personnel involved in gathering evidence at a crime scene must wear powder-free gloves.

Multiple-Choice Questions

1. Serology is the analysis of the properties and effects of:
    a. blood, urine, tissues, organs, and sweat
    b. semen, blood, saliva, sweat, and fecal matter
    c. DNA, blood, urine, sweat, and saliva
    d. none of the above

2. At the crime scene, the most frequently encountered biological stains are:
    a. urine, blood, and sweat
    b. blood, saliva, and sweat
    c. blood, seminal fluid, and saliva
    d. none of the above

3. Toxicology is the study of:
    a. DNA and blood to determine the presence of drugs or poisons
    b. body fluids to determine the presence of drugs or poisons
    c. organs and tissues to determine the presence of drugs or poisons
    d. body fluids, tissues, and organs to determine the presence of drugs or poisons

4. A *confirmatory test* for the presence of drugs or poisons is done:
    a. at the crime lab using a GC/MS
    b. at the crime scene by the CSI
    c. at the crime lab using alternative light sources
    d. at the crime scene by a forensic scientist

5. Physical evidence that can provide a timeline indicating drug use over a long period is:
    a. urine
    b. hair
    c. blood
    d. perspiration

6. Who discovered the first deoxyribonucleic acid (DNA) "fingerprints?"
    a. Sir Daniel Moeser
    b. Sir Alex Baldwin
    c. Sir Alec Jeffreys
    d. Sir Alan Jefferson

7. The Combined DNA Index System (CODIS) was established by:
    a.   ATF
    b.   ICE
    c.   FBI
    d.   INS

8. A _____ test is conducted at the crime scene to indicate the possibility of blood.
    a.   presumptive
    b.   initial
    c.   first
    d.   blood

9. Semen is composed of approximately _____ percent seminal fluid.
    a.   75
    b.   50
    c.   80
    d.   95

10. _____ is/are a substance that is present in semen and NOT found in any other body fluid.
    a.   Prostate specific antigen (PSA)
    b.   Deoxyribonucleic acid (DNA)
    c.   Antibodies
    d.   Blood type

11. Sperm heads detected in living persons have been detected for up to _____ days in the vaginal cavity
    a.   10
    b.   four
    c.   seven
    d.   two

12. Urine is primarily composed of:
    a.   blood and water
    b.   water and perspiration
    c.   seminal fluid and blood
    d.   salts and water

13. When lit with alternate or forensic light sources, blood appears _____ in color.
    a.   red
    b.   black
    c.   blue
    d.   green

14.   _____ is a chemiluminescent compound used to determine the presence of blood in the absence of visual stains, but is affected by household bleach.
    a.   Fluorescein
    b.   DNA
    c.   Luminol
    d.   Alternative light source

Discussion Questions

1.   Generally, what is forensic biology? Specifically, explain what the study of serology entails.

2.   What is the origin of deoxyribonucleic acid (DNA), and why it considered an "individual" characteristic of a person? Why has DNA been accepted in courts?

3.   What is CODIS, and why is it useful?

4.   When investigating a sexual assault, what are the unique procedures that should be followed, and why are they important?

7 Blood Spatter Evidence

Because blood is one of the most frequently encountered substances at a crime scene, its importance must not be underestimated. The position and shape of bloodstains may provide information about the circumstances of a crime. Trained bloodstain pattern analysts can interpret shape, location, size, and directionality at crime scenes that involve bloodshed. As more technicians are being certified, a wealth of information in the form of bloodstains is beginning to be utilized in the reconstruction of the events that occurred. A bloodstain pattern analyst (BPA) can provide many leads for the investigator.

Learning Objectives

1. Understand what a bloodstain pattern analyst (BPA) is.
2. Describe what *surface tension* is and how it relates to a drop of blood.
3. Explain the different blood spatter patterns on nonporous surfaces and rough surfaces.
4. List different conclusions a CSI can obtain from an analysis of blood spatter, and briefly explain each.
5. List the different types of impact spatter, and briefly explain each.
6. Name the unique types of blood spatter associated with gunshot wounds, and briefly describe each.
7. List and explain the four categories of bloodstains.
8. Explain what circumstances contribute to the "drying time" for blood.
9. Describe what specific information a BPA can provide the CSI, given adequate documentation.
10. Describe how a bloodstain is investigated. What measurements are required?
11. Explain the proper techniques for photographing bloodstains at a crime scene.

Key Terms

Bloodstain pattern analysis
Cast-off patterns
Contact stains
Directionality
Impact spatter
Passive stains
Point of convergence
Point or area of impact
Transfer stain
Wipe patterns

Chapter Outline

I.   Bloodstains

    A.   Passive

    B.   Initial locating of bloodstains

II.   Bloodstain Pattern Analysis

    A.   Basic interpretation of bloodstains
       1.   Shapes
       2.   Location
       3.   Distribution pattern(s)

    B.   Key objectives
       1.   Position of victim
       2.   Position of assailant
       3.   Type of weapon
       4.   Number of blows
       5.   Movement of victim/assailant after bloodshed

III. Blood Spatter

    A.   Drops of blood—free-falling on flat and rough surfaces
       1.   Surface tension
       2.   Nonporous surfaces—smooth and hard
          a.   Very little spatter
          b.   Circular
       3.   Rough surfaces
          a.   Irregular shape
          b.   Serrated/spiny edges

B.   Drops of blood—free-falling—angled surface
1.   90 degrees (no angle)
2.   More/less than 90 degrees
a.   Oval or elongated
b.   Uniqueness of seven-foot drop
c.   Examining edges of bloodstain

C.   Velocity of force
1.   Smaller force (slow-moving) = larger spatter size
2.   Greater force (faster-moving) = small spatter size
3.   Types of impact spatter
a.   Low velocity (less than 5 fps)
b.   Medium velocity (5-25 fps)
c.   High velocity (more than 25 fps)
d.   Gunshot spatter
(1)   Back spatter
(2)   Blowback spatter
(3)   Forward spatter (exit wound)

IV.   Bloodstain Categories

A.   Passive (drops)

B.   Impact and projected spatter (splashes, cast-off, gushing)

C.   Transfer bloodstain (wet surface in contact with another surface)

D.   Miscellaneous (void, fly spot, bubble rings)

D.   Drying time (humidity, temperature), perimeter to inward

V.   Measuring Techniques of Bloodstains

A.   Base of bloodstain to point of convergence (area of origin)

B.   Width and length—angle of impact

C.   Create a three-dimensional model to determine if a victim was standing, lying down, or sitting

VI.   Photographing the Scene

A.   Use overall, mid-range, and close up

B.   Mid-range shows relationship of stain to floor, corner of room, ceiling, etc.

C.   Close-up shows pattern of stain

True/False Questions

1. The average male has five to six liters of blood in his body.

2. The average female has approximately three to four liters of blood in her body.

3. The consensus is that a normal-sized individual must lose about 40 percent of the total volume of blood in order to produce irreversible shock and death.

4. Passive bloodstains are created by blunt force.

5. Regardless of the distance a free-falling drop of blood falls, it maintains its spherical shape.

6. When a drop of blood strikes a nonporous, smooth, and hard surface, it will create a large spatter.

7. Blood drops falling at a 90-degree angle will produce a circular stain of equal width and length.

8. Blood free-falling at more than seven feet in distance will not increase the diameter of the bloodstain.

9. When examining the edges of a bloodstains, the narrow end (or tail) of the stain usually points in the direction of travel.

10. A small or slow-moving force will create a smaller spatter size.

11. Bloodstains smaller than a freely forming drop are referred to as impact spatter.

12. With gunshots, there is only one type of spatter that will be created.

13. The category of bloodstain that is created by an arterial spurt of blood is an impact or projected spatter stain.

Multiple-Choice Questions

1. Bloodstain pattern analysis is the examination of the:
    a.   distribution patterns, size, and shapes
    b.   location, distribution patterns, and shapes
    c.   size, location, and shapes
    d.   shapes, location, and size

2. The average male has _____ to _____ liters of blood in his body:
    a.   four; five
    b.   three; four
    c.   five; six
    d.   six; seven

3. The average female has _____ to _____ liters of blood in his body:
    a.   four; five
    b.   three; four
    c.   five; six
    d.   six; seven

4. The consensus is that a normal-sized individual must lose about _____ percent of the total volume of blood in order to produce irreversible shock and death.
    a.   30
    b.   50
    c.   40
    d.   60

5. A free-falling drop of blood forms a sphere and maintains that shape due to the force that pulls the surface molecules of a liquid toward the interior. This force creates:
    a.   circular tendency
    b.   surface force
    c.   round syndrome
    d.   surface tension

6. A surface that is smooth and hard will create:
    a.   little, if any, spatter
    b.   more spatter than a rough surface
    c.   irregular stains with serrated or spiny edges
    d.   none of the above

7. Blood drops falling at a 90-degree angle will produce:
    a. a stain of unequal width and length
    b. a stain of equal width but unequal length
    c. a circular stain of equal width and length
    d. a circular stain of equal width but unequal length

8. At distances less than seven feet, the size or diameter of the bloodstain will _____ with the distance from where it originates to where it falls.
    a. increase
    b. decrease
    c. be the same as
    d. none of the above

9. The size of a spatter can be examined to indicate the velocity of the force that was applied. If a _____ force is involved, the spatter size will be _____.
    a. larger; larger
    b. smaller; smaller
    c. larger; smaller
    d. smaller; larger

10. Gunshots may produce two different sets of spatter:
    a. gravity and blowback
    b. blowback and forward
    c. exit and entrance
    d. none of the above

11. The four categories of bloodstains are:
    a. passive, impact, free-falling, and transfer
    b. free-falling, impact, passive, and miscellaneous
    d. transfer, impact, passive, and miscellaneous
    d. miscellaneous, impact, free-falling, and transfer

Discussion Questions

1. Discuss the characteristics of "blood spatter." Explain what can cause the spatter to be different given the same amount of blood.

2. Discuss the importance of photographing bloodstains at a crime scene. Specifically, what should the photographs capture?

3. Is there a need for the crime scene investigator to include a "diagram or sketch" if photographs are properly taken. If so, why?

8 Firearms and Toolmark Evidence

Establishing linkages between suspect, victim, and crime scene is important in every crime scene investigation. Associating bullets or other projectiles with the weapon that fired them is another type of linkage in the field of forensic evidence. Similarly, connecting a tool with the unique marks created by it can establish corroborating evidence that can lead to identification of the perpetrator of a crime. This is the key to firearms and toolmark investigations: when a bullet travels through the barrel of a gun, unique markings (striations, known as lands and grooves) are created on the surface of the bullet. These striations meet the definition of a toolmark, that is, an impression made on a softer surface (the bullet) by a tool or other object with a harder surface (the barrel's lands and grooves).

Firearms and toolmark examiners use comparison microscopes to complete forensic assessments of characteristics that are unique to a specific weapon or tool. Irregularities, impressions, abrasions, and striations are significant individual markings that provide sufficient evidence that the mark was made by a certain weapon or tool to the exclusion of all others.

Learning Objectives

1. Understand the difference between a handgun and long gun.
2. Describe the difference between *firearms identification* and *ballistics*.
3. List and explain what a firearms examiner can potentially provide to the CSI.
4. Describe what components all cartridge ammunition will include.
5. Describe how a bullet is fired.
6. Understand several types of bullets used today.

7. Explain why the marks (striations) on fired bullets are called "fingerprints."
8. Describe the class characteristics of bullets.
9. Describe the class characteristics of a discharged cartridge.
10. What are the three conclusions a firearms examiner can render concerning a suspect weapon and recovered bullets
11. Understand how to locate, collect, package, and account for firearms, bullets, and cartridges.
12. Describe what a *sodium rhodizonate* test is used for.
13. Briefly describe the basic effects that occur when a cylindrical object (bullet) impacts a surface.
14. Understand what concentric and radial glass fractures are, how to identify them, and what they reveal.
15. Understand how ballistic trajectory is determined and the use of a laser protractor kit and laser trajectory kit.
16. Explain basically how the firing distance is established.
17. Describe what the absence of gun powder residue may reveal.
18. Describe what purpose is served by the NIBIN.
19. Explain what GSR is and what it may reveal to the CSI.
20. List and describe the three types of tool marks.

Key Terms

Ballistics
Compression toolmarks
Concentric fractures
Cutting toolmarks
Gunshot residue (GSR)
Lands and grooves
Laser protractor kit
National Integrated Ballistics Information Network (NIBIN)
Radial fractures
Sliding toolmarks
Striations
Tattooing
Trajectory

Chapter Outline

I.   Guns

    A.   Handguns
        1.   Revolvers, pistols
        2.   Designed for one-handed operation

    B.   Long guns
        1.   Rifles, shotguns
        2.   Designed for two-handed operation

III.   Firearms Identification

    A.   Type and caliber of weapon

    B.   Angle and distance of gun fired

    C.   Sequence of events

    D.   Functionality of weapon

IV.   Bullets and Cartridges

    A.   Bullets
        1.   Lead—disadvantages
        2.   Semi-jacketed
        3.   Full metal jacket—advantages
        4.   Shotgun slugs/shot

    B.   Cartridge
        1.   Projectile
        2.   Powder
        3.   Primer
        4.   Casing

    C.   National Integrated Ballistics Information Network (NIBIN)

V.   Class versus Individual Characteristics

    A.   Class—bullet
        1.   Caliber
        2.   Number of lands and grooves
        3.   Width of lands and grooves
        4.   Direction of twist

    B.   Class—cartridge
        1.   Caliber
        2.   Firing pin location, size, and shape
        3.   Primer type
        4.   Extractor marks

C. Individual—bullet
1. Striations
2. Other irregularities, impressions, or abrasions

VI. Conclusions of a Firearms Examiner

A. The bullet was fired by the suspect gun

B. Exclude the suspect weapon

C. Class characteristics match but are inconclusive

VII. Locating, Collecting, Packaging, and Submission of Evidence

A. Locating
1. Make weapon safe
2. Examine for trace evidence
3. Sodium rhodizonate test

B. Collecting
1. Document location with photograph, sketches, and notes
2. Indicate position of cylinder (revolver) and chamber bullets removed
3. Document safety position if applicable

C. Packaging
1. Use sturdy cardboard boxes and plastic wire ties
2. Cylinder of revolver secured in open position, pistol-slide locked in open position
3. Bullets or fragments should be packaged separately in paper and a plastic bag, then in a rigid container

D. Submission
1. Ensure that every item is itemized separately
2. Note if package contains live ammunition

VIII. Trajectories and Measurements

A. Trajectory
1. Identifying shooters position, movements, sequence of shots
2. Bullets passing through at 90 degrees
3. More/less than 90 degrees
a. Elliptical hole
b. Fracture pattern more to the side of hole on which bullet is traveling, less on side bullet came from
4. Laser protractor kit
5. Laser trajectory kit

B. Measurement
    1. Distance of shooter to victim
        a. Examine entrance wound
        b. Impact marks
        c. GSR
    2. Compare to test patterns using same weapon and ammunition

IX. Ballistic Damage Evidence

   A. Sodium rhodizonate test

   B. Establishing entrance/exit holes

   C. Sequence of events

   D. Presence of GSR

   E. When a bullet impacts a surface
       1. Compression
       2. Tension

   F. Glass
       1. Laminate curl (windshield)
       2. Concentric fracture
       3. Radial fracture
       4. Scrape fingernail on surface

X. Toolmark Categories

   A. Compression
       1. Most common
       2. When a tool is pressed into a softer material

   B. Cutting
       1. Found on chains, bolts, hasps, etc.
       2. Usually a bolt cutter used

   C. Sliding
       1. Tool slides along another surface leaving parallel striations
       2. Use of a screwdriver or pry bar on edge of door to find locking mechanism

XI. Serial Numbers

   A. Typically are impressed into metal object (gun barrel, engine block)

   B. When numbers are removed by grinding, scraping, or drilling, chemical tests are used:
       1. Magnaflux, chemical etching, and ultrasonic cavitating
       2. Heat processes

True/False Questions

1.   When a bullet travels through the barrel of a gun, unique markings called striations are created.

2.   There are two categories of firearms—revolvers and pistols.

3.   *Ballistics* means the study of a projectile in motion.

4.   *Firearms identification* and *ballistics* are synonymous.

5.   All types of cartridge ammunition include a projectile, powder, primer, and cartridge or shell casing as the main components.

6.   Bullets are generally made from lead, which is a hard and lightweight metal.

7.   Bullets made from lead can easily cause jamming in magazine-fed semi-automatic handguns.

8.   Firearms identification is primarily concerned with the determination of whether a bullet, cartridge case, or other ammunition was discharged, extracted, or ejected from a specific firearm.

9.   Research and studies over the years have shown that two different firearms will occasionally produce the same unique marks (striations) on fired bullets and cartridge cases.

10.   Class characteristics of bullets include caliber, number of lands and grooves, and width of lands and grooves.

11.   Class characteristics of cartridges include primer type, caliber, and firing pin location.

12.   According to the text, when preparing for transportation from the crime scene, the cylinder of a revolver should be secured in the closed position.

13.   The portion of the cartridge that is extracted and ejected from the chamber after the bullet has been fired is referred to as the discharged shell casing.

14.   According to the text, a firearm recovered under water should be allowed to dry completely before being packaged for transportation.

15. According to the text, when possible, bullets that are embedded in wood or some other material should be carefully removed before transporting to the lab.

16. Simple chemical tests for lead and other metals associated with bullets can be performed on the damaged sites if there is a question as to whether a hole or impact site was actually made by the bullet.

17. When a cylindrical object impacts another surface, the energy on the impact side will cause the impacted surface to come under tension.

18. The two most commonly seen fracture patterns that occur when glass is broken are concentric and radial fractures.

19. Concentric fractures occur on the impact side of the glass.

20. When a bullet passes through glass, radial fractures occur on the impact side of the glass.

21. The nationwide computer database (NIBIN) that contains unique characteristics or "signatures" of expended bullets and cartridge cases is maintained by the FBI and Secret Service.

22. Gunshot residue may be found at the site of the entrance wound.

23. Tests have shown that gunshot residue deposits are detectable on a subject's hands for approximately 12 hours.

24. Toolmark impressions can be divided into three general categories: compression, cutting, and sliding.

25. When a serial number is impressed into a metal object, the metal underneath is compressed and hardened.

26 One method a crime lab can use to recover the original serial number that has been removed from a gun is ultrasonic cavitation.

Multiple-Choice Questions

1. There are two categories of firearms:
   a. handguns and long guns
   b. pistols and shotguns
   c. pistols and revolvers
   d. rifles and shotguns

2. All types of cartridge ammunition include:
   a.   projectile, bullet, powder, and primer
   b.   primer, projectile, powder, and cartridge/shell casing
   c.   bullet, primer, projectile, and cartridge/shell casing
   d.   none of the above

3. Bullets are generally made from:
   a.   steel
   b.   iron
   c.   lead
   d.   any hard metal

4. Some types of bullets include:
   a.   ball, wad-cutter, full metal jacket
   b.   semi-metal jacket, ball, elongated
   c.   full metal jacket, elongated, ball
   d.   ball, hard-point, wad-cutter

5. Class characteristics of bullets include:
   a.   caliber, number of lands and grooves, length of bullet
   b.   lands and grooves, caliber, degree of twist
   c.   degree of twist, lands and grooves, firing-pin size, and shape
   d.   caliber, firing-pin location, and degree of twist

6. Which is NOT a conclusion a firearms examiner can render concerning the comparison of a suspect weapon to recovered bullets?
   a.   The bullet was fired by the suspect gun.
   b.   The suspect gun is excluded.
   c.   The results are inconclusive.
   d.   all of the above

7. The portion of the cartridge that is extracted and ejected from the chamber of a pistol after the bullet has been fired is referred to as the:
   a.   spent shell casing
   b.   fired shell casing
   c.   discharged shell casing
   d.   none of the above

8. According to the text, whenever a shot pattern is present at the crime scene and cannot be submitted to the laboratory, a _____ photograph should be taken:
   a.   scaled
   b.   enlarged
   c.   detailed
   d.   black and white

9. A firearm recovered under water should be:
   a. completely dried first, then packaged for transportation
   b. sealed in a plastic bag and submerged in the same water
   c. immediately sealed in a plastic bag before drying
   d. allowed to dry and then sealed in a cardboard box

10. When possible, bullets that are embedded should be removed:
    a. using a knife
    b. using a special spoon type instrument
    c. by the crime lab
    d. by the CSI only

11. A simple _____ test can be performed on a damaged site if there is a question as to whether a hole was made by a bullet.
    a. chemical
    b. stress
    c. impact
    d. pattern

12. When performing a sodium rhodizonate test for lead, a _____ color will appear if trace amounts of lead are present.
    a. dark orange to red
    b. dark blue to violet
    c. dark gray to light black
    d. dark red to purplish

13. The two most commonly seen glass fracture patterns that occur when glass is broken are:
    a. radial and circular
    b. round and radial
    c. concentric and radial
    d. oblong and concentric

14. The National Integrated Ballistics Information Network (NIBIN) is maintained by the:
    a. CIA and the FBI
    b. FBI and the ATF
    c. ATF and the ICE
    d. FBI and the DEA

15. Tests have shown that gunshot residue is not detectable on a subject's hands after _____ have elapsed from the time a gun was fired.
    a.   four to six hours
    b.   two to four hours
    c.   three to five hours
    d.   five to seven hours

16. Toolmark impressions can be divided into three general categories:
    a.   compression, scraping, cutting
    b.   cutting, compression, sliding
    c.   sliding, hacking, cutting
    d.   compression, sliding, scraping

17. When a serial number is impressed in a metal object, the metal underneath is:
    a.   compressed and hardened
    b.   condensed and compressed
    c.   hardened and embossed
    d.   compressed and molded

Discussion Questions

1.   What is meant by the term *ballistics*? Discuss the possible information that can be obtained from a handgun or long gun and its projectile.

2.   What characteristics make each firearm unique?

3.   What is a laser trajectory rod kit, and what is its use?

4.   What is the significance of the presence or absence of gun powder residue?

 **9** **Arson and Explosives**

Evidence may be contaminated or cross-contaminated by volatile accelerants or the effects of fire suppression and overhauling. Precautions must be taken to protect against further contamination or increased hazards to your health. It may be necessary to secure the fire scene, entering only after environmental concerns have been identified and addressed, so do not begin this investigation without proper clearance from health, safety, and fire officials.

Learning Objectives

1. Define arson.
2. Describe the unusual circumstances a CSI faces when responding to a potential arson fire in progress.
3. Understand how an arson or explosive crime scene is processed.
4. Explain how the area of origin of the fire is located.
5. Describe what the *fire triangle* is.
6. Describe how fire normally spreads.
7. Describe what the modes of heat transfer are.
8. Describe the three primary reasons for investigating fire scenes.
9. Describe what the CSI should focus on if arson is suspected to be covering up a prior crime.
10. According to the FBI, describe what the motives are for purposely setting fires.
11. Define *serial* fires.
12. Describe the four possible classifications of the cause of a fire.
13. Understand the resistance of the human body to be totally reduced to ashes.
14. Explain how a human body can be identified when consumed in a fire.
15. Understand what a pugilistic stance is and what causes it in the circumstances of a fire

16. Describe the *explosives incident system* and who maintains it.
17. Describe what an explosion is.
18. List the three types of explosions and the two broad categories of explosions.
19 Explain what events occur when there is an explosion.
20. Describe how the area of origin of an explosion is located.
21. Briefly explain how residue samples should be collected from an explosion site.

Key Terms

Area of origin
Burn patterns
CBRNE
Fire triangle
High explosives
IEDs
Low explosives
National Fire Protection Association (NFPA)
Serial fires
Spoliation
Trailers or streamers

Chapter Outline

I.   Initial Response to Scene

    A.   Safety first

    B.   Environmental concerns

    C.   Responding agencies will have different priorities

II.   Initial Processing of Potential Crime Scene

    A.   Start from area of least damage to area of most damage

    B.   Goal to locate area of origin

III. Fire Triangle

    A.   Heat

    B.   Fuel

    C.   Oxygen

IV. The Spreading Fire

  A. Burn pattern
     1. Nature of flame
     2. Heat
     3. Smoke movements
     4. Damage pattern—floors, walls, ceilings, etc.

  B. Heat transfer
     1. Convection
     2. Conduction
     3. Radiation
     4. Ventilation

V. Why Investigate Fire Scenes

  A. Locate point of origin
     1. Establish the cause of fire
     2. Determine if crime committed

  B. Safety
     1. Product defect
     2. Misuse of product

  C. State 7 Local codes
     1. Violation by inhabitant
     2. Violation by builder/owner

VI. Motives

  A. Vandalism

  B. Excitement

  C. Revenge

  D. Profit

  E. Extremism

  F. Conceal another crime

VII. Arson as Cover-up

  A. Document pre-fire conditions

  B. Identify all electrical devices and ignitable materials

  C. Locate smoke detectors and determine whether they are in working condition

  D. Look for missing important documents, valuable items, etc.

  E. Determine if the amount of damage was consistent with the potential cause

VIII.   Collection of Arson Evidence

    A.   National Fire Protection Association (NFPA)

    B.   Locating ignitable substances residue (ISR)
        1.   Certified accelerant detection K-9s (ACDs)
        2.   Electronic detectors
        3.   Flame ionization (FID)
        4.   Fourier transform infrared spectroscopy (FTIR)
        5.   Portable gas chromatography/mass spectrometry
        6.   Forensic light source/alternate light source
        7.   Field flame/burn tests

IX.   Classifications of causes of fire

    A.   Accidental

    B.   Incendiary

    C.   Natural

    D.   Undetermined

X.   Recovery of Burned Human Bodies

    A.   All recovered bodies should be autopsied to determine cause of death

    B.   Document (photo, sketch, notes) body before removal of site

    C.   A systematic search of the area the body was found and all surrounding areas for forensic evidence

XI.   Identification of Burned Bodies

    A.   Visual—least reliable

    B.   Clothing and jewelry

    C.   X-rays—most reliable
        1.   Examination of bones
        2.   Examination of teeth

XII. Causes of Death

    A.   Smoke inhalation

    B.   Burns

    C.   Trauma
        1.   GSW, stabbing
        2.   Carbon monoxide poison, heart attack, etc.

    D.   Determine whether accidental, homicide, natural, undetermined, suicide

XIII. Bomb Scene and Explosives

    A.   Explosives Incident System (EIS)
       1.   Database of information concerning theft or use of explosives
       2.   Maintained by ATF

    B.   Types of explosives
       1.   Mechanical
       2.   Chemical
       3.   Nuclear

    C.   Categories
       1.   Low
          a.   Burn rather than explode
          b.   Black powder
          c.   Smokeless powder
          d.   Usually confined in container and initiated by fuses
       2.   High
          a.   Primary
             (1)   Detonate forcible—sensitive to heat
             (2)   Sensitive to shock
          b.   Secondary
             (1)   Dynamite,
             (2)   Military grade (C-4 and TNT)
          c.   Tertiary
             (1)   Ammonium nitrate
             (2)   Urea nitrate and fuel oil

    D.   Events of an explosion
       1.   Blast pressure effect (shock wave)
       2.   Air rushes back into void (causes tertiary blast injuries)
       3.   Shrapnel (secondary blast injuries)

    E.   Locating explosive devices an evidence collecting
       1.   Look for crater
       2.   Collect soil samples of origin and surrounding areas
       3.   Collect residue sample
          a.   Dry cotton gauze
          b.   Dry cotton gauze dampened with methanol/ethanol

True/False Questions

1.   According to the text, overall scene security and the safety of all personnel are of paramount importance during an active fire.

2.   As with all investigations, the CSI must work from the center of the fire scene outward.

3. Fire is a chemical process that requires heat, fuel, and oxygen.

4. Burn patterns indicate the nature of flame, heat, and smoke movements within a structure.

5. The three modes of heat transfer are convection, conduction, and radiation.

6. In the flame zone, the pattern will resemble a V.

7. Ventilation will impact the spread of the fire and creates intensity and movement patterns.

8. Fire patterns will be found only on vertical surfaces because heat rises.

9. Two or more incendiary fires attributed to an individual or group are classified as serial fires.

10. Arson is the willful and malicious burning of another's property or of one's own property for some illegal purpose.

11. Arson investigators must master standards set by the National Fire Protection Association (NFPA).

12. One proven way to locate minute amounts of ignitable substances residue (ISR) is the use of Accelerant Detection K-9s (ACDs).

13. A type of electronic chemical detector used to locate possible ISR at a fire scene that draws the suspect vapor over a heated metal coil is the metal oxide transistor detector.

14. When collecting evidence at a fire scene, it is acceptable to absorb liquid samples with clean, sterile cotton balls or gauze pads and then seal them in an airtight container.

15. There are four possible classifications of the cause of a fire: accidental, incendiary, natural, and undetermined.

16. For a body to be reduced to ashes takes several hours of exposure to temperatures ranging from 1,800 to 2,000 degrees Fahrenheit.

17. According to the text, visual identification is the most reliable means of verifying a body.

18. A forensic anthropologist can determine if bones are human or animal.

19. The manner of death of a person in a fire can be homicide, natural, undetermined, or suicide.

20. The FBI maintains the Explosives Incident System, which is a centralized repository of information concerning the theft or use of explosives.

21. The two broad categories of explosives are high explosives and low explosives.

22. Low explosives burn rather than explode.

23. Primary explosives are generally used to manufacture blasting caps and are not often used as the main charge.

24. When explosives detonate, air rushes back into the void created by the positive pressure causing tertiary blast injuries from blunt trauma.

25. The presence of a crater will indicate the origin of the blast, regardless of whether high or low explosives were used.

26. According to the text, for every questioned sample at a fire scene, a control sample must be collected and submitted for analysis.

Multiple-Choice Questions

1. The CSI should investigate a fire scene:
    a. from the center of scene, outward
    b. from area of least destruction to area of most destruction
    c. from edge of crime scene, inward
    d. from area fire is first extinguished to area where fire is last extinguished

2. The *fire triangle* is:
    a. gas, heat, CO^2
    b. heat, CO^2, fuel
    c. heat, fuel, oxygen
    d. oxygen, explosive device, nitrogen

3. _____ indicate the nature of flame, heat, and smoke movements within a structure.
    a. Burn patterns
    b. Burn trails
    c. Burn marks
    d. Burn plumes

4. Fire normally follows:
    a.   horizontal movements
    b.   vertical movements
    c.   the path of most resistance
    d.   the path of least resistance

5. The three modes of heat transfer are:
    a.   conception, conduction, radiation
    b.   conduction, radiation, intensity
    c.   convection, conduction, radiation
    d.   gas, smoke, flames

6. According to the text, fire patterns are most often observed on:
    a.   walls, floors, and ceilings
    b.   ceilings, windows, and doors
    c.   exterior doors, ceilings, and floors
    d.   whatever area is closest to the origin of fire

7. Fire patterns that are created when ignitable substances are deliberately connected from one area to another are called:
    a.   connecting paths
    b.   fire connectors
    c.   trailers or streamers
    d.   horizontal and vertical patterns

8. One of the three primary reasons for investigating a fire scene is:
    a.   the motive for the fire
    b.   the person who set the fire
    c.   the point of origin of the fire
    d.   the fire patterns of the fire

9. The CSI is most likely to be involved in an incendiary fire investigation of a fire started because of:
    a.   revenge of injustice
    b.   concealment of another crime
    c.   excitement
    d.   extremists

10. According to the text, the definition of *arson* is:
    a.   willful and malicious burning of another's property or of one's own property for some illegal purpose
    b.   willful and malicious burning of another's property for some illegal purpose
    c.   willful setting of a fire for the purpose of destruction of property
    d.   none of the above

11. The organization that has established standards that dictate the knowledge, skills, and abilities that arson investigators must master is the:
    a. National Fire Prevention Association
    b. National Association for Fire Prevention
    c. National Fire Protection Association
    d. National Association for Fire Protection

12. The acronym CBRNE stands for:
    a. crime, biological, radiological, natural, explosive
    b. crime, biological, radiant, nuclear, expanded
    c. chemical, biological, radiological, nuclear, explosive
    d. chemical, biological, radiant, nuclear, explosive

13. A portable field version of a highly respected laboratory identification system for identifying ignitable substance residues is the:
    a. flame ionization detector
    b. accelerant detection K-9s
    c. gas chromatography/mass spectrometry
    d. catalytic combustion detector

14. Through detailed crime scene processing, there are four possible classifications of the cause of a fire:
    a. accidental, incendiary, natural, undetermined
    b. accidental, incendiary, natural, purposeful
    c. revengeful, incendiary, natural, undetermined
    d. none of the above

15. Studies reveal that in order for a body to be reduced to ashes, temperatures ranging from _____ to _____ degrees Fahrenheit must be maintained for several hours.
    a. 1,000; 2,000
    b. 1,500; 1800
    c. 1,800; 2200
    d. 1,899; 2,000

16. According to the text, the four methods or techniques for identifying burned humans are:
    a. visual, forensic anthropologist, bone structure, clothing/jewelry
    b. forensic anthropologist, clothing/jewelry, visual, X-rays
    c. X-rays, MS/GAMMA test, visual, clothing/jewelry
    d. visual, X-rays, position of body, clothing/jewelry

17. The agency that maintains the Explosives Incident System is the:
    a.   FBI
    b.   ICE
    c.   DEA
    d.   ATF

18. The two broad categories of explosives are:
    a.   black powder and smokeless powder
    b.   black powder and primary
    c.   low and high
    d.   primary and secondary

19. The presence of a _____ will indicate the origin of the blast.
    a.   crater
    b.   burn pattern
    c.   plume
    d.   igniter

20. For every questioned sample taken from a fire scene, a _____ sample must be collected and submitted for analysis.
    a.   second
    b.   confirmation
    c.   control
    d.   identical

Discussion Questions

1.   When investigating arson, what is the primary initial question the arson investigator is trying to answer?

2.   Discuss what is meant by *burn patterns* and what characteristics affect them.

3.   What are the different types of explosives? Explain each. Describe the different *categories* of explosions.

10 The Electronic Crime Scene

Computers and technology have permeated our everyday environment, and it is impossible to measure the impact the Internet has on today's world. Because technology is abundant in our lifestyles, so is digital evidence. The criminal element is also utilizing technology to avoid getting caught and to commit even more offenses. Advances in digital capacity far outpace the capabilities of law enforcement officers to detect and apprehend the perpetrators. It is more likely than not that those involved in criminal operations are utilizing cell phones, computers, and the Internet.

Forensic evidence examiners will reconstruct the cybercrime scene utilizing the photographs, sketches, and written documentation provided by the CSI. They will attempt to recreate the network connections and begin to analyze the data that is stored on the duplicate of the hard drive. The original data files are not used for examination so as not to destroy the original evidence.

Learning Objectives

1. Describe what *digital evidence* is and why it is sometimes called an *electronic fingerprint*.
2. Understand what ISPs are and how they can assist the CSI.
3. Describe some types of digital crime.
4. Describe sources of digital evidence in addition to IP addresses.
5. Describe what is meant by *identity theft* and what it includes.
6. Define *spyware* and explain how it works.
7. Describe the PROTECT Act of 2003 and the provisions it contains.
8. Describe what is meant by *cyberstalking*.

9. Understand what is meant by *cybertailing*.
10. List the common motives of a hacker.
11. Describe what is meant by *phishing*.
12. Describe what a CSI should consider when processing an electronic crime scene.
13. Describe what is meant by *crime scene staging*.

Key Terms

Computer crime
Crime scene staging
Cybercrime
Cyberstalking
Cybertailing
Digital evidence
Digital forensics
Encryption
Hacker
Identity theft
Internet protocol (IP)
Internet service providers (ISPs)
Phishing
PROTECT Act of 2003
Script kiddie
Spyware
Uniform resource locator (URL)

Chapter Outline

I.   Digital Evidence at a Crime Scene

    A. Collected with assistance of a digital evidence examiner

    B. Cell phones, PDAs, wireless laptops

II. How electronic information is transmitted

    A. Internet Service Providers (ISPs)

    B. Internet protocol (IP) addresses
        1. Dynamic
        2. Assigned to a computer upon connection
        3. Log created

III.   Other Digital Evidence

    A.   Computer-based diaries

    B.   Buddy lists

    C.   Spreadsheets

    D.   Web browsers' history of sites visited

    E.   Downloaded files

IV.   Types of Digital Crimes

    A.   Identity theft
       1.   48 percent of all fraud complaints
       2.   Low risk of being caught
          a.   Credit card fraud
          b.   Utilities fraud
          c.   Bank fraud
          d.   Loans
          e.   Government documents
       3.   Individuals do not take precautionary measures to protect their information
       4.   Spyware—monitors Internet activities to gain personal information and pass to third party

    B.   Crimes Against Children
       1.   Solicitation of minors for sex
       2.   Child pornography
          a.   PROTECT Act of 2003
          b.   Chat rooms
       3.   Not all countries have same laws

    C.   Cyberstalking
       1.   Typical stalking with Internet features added
       2.   Cybertailing used to combat cyberstalking

    D.   Hackers
       1.   Motives
          a.   Revenge
          b.   Profit (phishing)
          c.   Pride
          d.   Curiosity

V.   Processing the Electronic Crime Scene

    A.   When possible, gain assistance from a digital evidence investigator

    B.   Photograph and document by notes/sketches all equipment and location of all cables, connections, and peripheral equipment

    C.   If power is off, do not turn on

    D.   Check all hardware for latent prints

    E.   If power is on
1. Photograph the screen
2. Make list of all files open
3. Download all open files to storage device
4. Document the system time and date
5. Document the actual time and date
6. Disconnect power cord from chassis, but do no not power down or shut down. Disconnect power cord from wall.
7. Seal all openings in the chassis with evidence tape
8. If laptop, remove battery
9. Disconnect cables
10. Remove chassis cover and photograph all interior

    F.   Software
1. Write-protect each disk
2. Check for physical damage
3. Check microwaves for software

    G.   Peripheral Equipment
1. Disconnect and package separately
2. Photograph and document where the equipment was connected
3. Collect all software/hardware manuals

    H.   Cell phones
1. Leave power in the same position as found
2. If possible, document call logs and photograph them
3. Collect all power cords, connection cables, etc.
4. Transport to lab immediately if power is left on

True/False Questions

1. Internet protocol (IP) addresses are assigned to specific users each time they sign on.

2. Identify theft comprises approximately 75 percent of all fraud complaints filed with the Federal Trade Commission.

3. Spyware is a self-installing software program that exploits infected computers by monitoring the Internet activities of the computer user and providing data to third parties.

4. Spyware is usually easily detected on computers because it make computers run faster than normal.

5. The PROTECT Act of 2003 modified federal pornography laws to define the possession of child pornography as being in possession of contraband.

6. Cybertailing is the process of following a perpetrator through various computer networks in an attempt to identify a suspect.

7. Phishing is an Internet fraud scheme that utilizes real web sites that look different from the original web sites of banks or credit card companies in an attempt to secure personal account information.

8. One of the special considerations when beginning to process a computer crime scene is the determination of whether the system is powered up when you arrive.

9. When beginning an investigation of a computer crime scene, all equipment should be powered up so a check of all systems can be accomplished.

10. When collecting software, the CSI should write-protect each disk.

11. After documentation of the computer is complete, the CSI should perform a system shutdown and prepare the computer for transportation.

12. The attempt to plant or fabricate digital evidence that will implicate someone else is called staging.

Multiple-Choice Questions

1. The type of evidence the CSI gets from investigating a computer crime scene is:
    a. analog
    b. electronic
    c. digital
    d. fingerprint

2. In reference to computers, ISP stands for:
    a. Internet Service Provider
    b. Internet Service Protocol
    c. Internet Serving Protection
    d. none of the above

3. Which is not a type of digital crime?
   a. identify theft
   b. pornography
   c. cyberstalking
   d. credit card fraud

4. Identify theft comprises approximately _____ of all fraud complaints.
   a. 50 percent
   b. 40 percent
   c. 60 percent
   d. 70 percent

5. The four crimes covered by the Identity Theft and Assumption Deterrence Act of 1998 are:
   a. Bank Fraud, Credit Card Fraud, Loans, Government Documents
   b. Government Documents, Bank Fraud, Internet Shopping, Credit Card Fraud
   c. Credit Card Fraud, Loans, Mortgage Shopping, Government Documents
   d. Bank Fraud, Credit Card Fraud, Loans, Telephone Numbers

6. Self-installing software programs that exploit infected computers by monitoring the Internet activities of the computer user and providing this data to third parties are called:
   a. monitoring software
   b. analyzing software
   c. spyware
   d. phishing software

7. The PROTECT Act of 2003 deals with what kind of crime?
   a. bank fraud
   b. government documents
   c. child pornography
   d. phishing

8. The process of following a perpetrator through various computer networks in an attempt to identify a suspect is called:
   a. cyberstalking
   b. phishing
   c. cybertailing
   d. tailgating

9. An Internet fraud scheme that utilizes fake web sites that look like the real sites of bank or credit card companies and attempts to secure personal account information is called:
    a. phishing
    b. cyberstalking
    c. cybertailing
    d. cybercrime

10. According to the text, when collecting software, you should _____ each disk prior to sealing it in a package.
    a. photograph
    b. write protect
    c. duplicate
    d. none of the above

11. According to the text, when should a system shutdown be performed on a computer that is powered up?
    a. after photographing is complete
    b. after all files have been copied
    c. never
    d. after all cables and peripheral equipment have been detached

12. Crime scene _____ occurs when perpetrators attempt to plant or fabricate digital evidence that will implicate someone else.
    a. staging
    b. phishing
    c. cyberstalking
    d. cybertailing

Discussion Questions

1. Define *identity theft,* and describe several ways it is accomplished.

2. Why do people become hackers? Explain each reason.

3. Describe the procedure for seizing a computer and its associated equipment.

 # Documentary Evidence

Documents recovered from a crime scene may often be a crucial form of physical evidence. Documentary evidence may include items that indicate motive, such as love letters, financial records, personal diaries, and threatening letters. Sometimes, documents found at a crime scene may yield information about other suspects, victims, and/or locations, such as maps, phone numbers, and indented writings on a pad of paper.

Learning Objectives

1. Describe the many types of questioned documents.
2. Understand how evidential paper documents should be handled and the preferred way to maintain chain of custody.
3. Describe the procedures for handling burned or charred documents.
4. Understand procedures for examining documents as set by the ASTM.
5. Describe destructive and nondestructive techniques of examining documents.
6. Describe the procedures used by handwriting identification experts.
7. Understand the constitutional issues when requiring handwriting exemplars.
8. Describe what is meant by simulated and imitation handwriting.
9. Describe how the ASTM identifies handwriting elements.
10. Describe specific analyses for signatures.
11. List the nine-item scale for expressing conclusions by the ASTM.
12. Describe how handwriting is used for criminal profiling.
13. Describe how handwriting is used for physical profiting.

Key Terms

ASTM (American Society for Testing and Materials)
Complexity of handwriting
ESDA (electrostatic detection apparatus)
Exemplars
Forensic linguistics
Graphology
Line quality
Simulated signature
Statement analysis
Thin-layer chromatography (TLC)
Trash marks

Chapter Outline

I.   Types of Documents Used for Evidence

    A.   Unquestioned documents
        1.   Authenticity not disputed
        2.   Identity of writer not disputed

    B.   Questioned documents
        1.   Counterfeit document
        2.   Forged document

II.   Handling and Recording Evidential Documents

    A.   Paper documents should be handled with white cotton gloves

    B.   Secure paper documents to minimize folding, handling, or impressions

    C.   Paper documents can be later tested for latent impressions, indentation, and fingerprints

    D.   Never use plastic sleeves because they trap moisture

    E.   If possible, do not write on documents. Seal document in envelope and put required information on envelope; write on envelope first and then put document inside.

    F.   Photograph all handwriting or drawings that cannot be removed

    G.   Always document by sketches and notes where the document was found

    H.   Burned or charred documents
        1.   Spray with fine mist of varnish
        2.   Place in box with loosely packed cotton
        3.   Do not mail

III.   Examining Documents—(ASTM)

    A.   Nondestructive Methods
       1.   Ultraviolet (UV) light
          a.   Detect chemical erasures
          b.   Detect different paper types in multi-page documents
       2.   Infrared (IR) light
          a.   Detect change in ink
          b.   Recover obliterated material (entry cross out with ink)
       3.   Side-lighting or oblique lighting
          a.   Helps make latent indentations visible
          b.   Especially helpful if document was under a pad of paper
       4.   Backlighting
          a.   Light placed behind document to make it more transparent
          b.   Assist visibility of writing if there are blacked-out or whited-out portions
          c.   Used to see watermarks
       5.   Electrostatic Detection Device
          a.   Develop patent fingerprints
          b.   More sophisticated than side or oblique lighting

    B.   Destructive Methods
       1.   Typical ninhydrin chemical
       2.   Anything that adds chemicals to document

IV.   Handwriting Documents

    A.   Must have an unquestioned or known writing sample
       1.   Best samples are from business documents
       2.   Checks, deeds, driver license, passport, etc.

    B.   No two people have identical handwriting nor are any two writings by same person exactly the same

    C.   Experts look for "patterns"

    D.   Identical writings (signatures) indicate potential of tracing or copying

    E.   Exemplars should be similar in composition to the questioned document

    F.   Never show the questioned document to suspect

    G.   Signatures should be written as fast as possible using both hands

    H.   Case law has established that requiring handwriting exemplars does not violate the Fourth or Fifth Amendments, nor does it require the presence of counsel

    I.   Simulation, imitation, and copying or digitally transferring a signature

J. ASTM elements for examining handwriting

K. ASTM scale for expressing conclusions of handwriting analysis
   1. Identification
   2. Strong probability
   3. Probable
   4. Indication
   5. No conclusion
   6. Indications did not
   7. Probably did not
   8. Strong probability did not
   9. Elimination

L. Criminal profiling

M. Physical profiling—age, gender, literacy occupation, health

N. Impulsivity handwriting

V. Forensic Linguistics, Statement Analysis, Handwriting

   A. Define forensic linguistics

   B. Define statement analysis

   C. Using handwriting signs of dishonesty with statement analysis

True/False Questions

1. A questioned document is one in which the authenticity of the document itself is in question or in which the identity of the writer is in question.

2. Documentary evidence may be questioned or unquestioned.

3. Handwriting or drawings that cannot be physically removed from the crime scene as evidence may be duplicated by hand.

4. Spraying a fine mist of clear varnish over charred documents in a box with loosely packed cotton may help prevent further deterioration of the document.

5. Documents should be examined and photographed prior to fingerprint development.

6. The American Society for Testing and Materials (ASTM) publishes recommended standards and procedures for examination of documents.

7. Both shortwave and longwave ultraviolet (UV) light can be used in examining and differentiating ink.

8. Infrared (IR) light can be used in examining and differentiating ink. Two nondestructive lighting techniques used for examining documents are oblique and transmitted lighting.

9. Electrostatic detection is a device used to determine the opacity of paper and visualizing watermarks.

10. A suspect's natural writing habits are more effectively demonstrated on what are known as normal-course-of-business documents such as rental agreements, mortgages, and deeds.

11. The same person will have the same handwriting about 20 percent of the time.

12. Two signatures that are exactly alike indicate that one of the signatures is a copy or tracing of an original signature.

13. Case law has established that the taking of handwriting exemplars for identification purposes is not a violation of the Fourth and Fifth Amendments to the U.S. Constitution.

14. When a person is required to submit handwriting samples, he or she has a constitutional right to have counsel present.

15. According to Huber and Headrick (1999), there are 21 "discriminating elements of handwriting."

16. The four categories of discriminating elements of handwriting according to Huber and Headrick (1999) are: style, consistency, execution, and accuracy.

17. Impulsivity in handwriting is seen through strong rightward movement, erratic and disorganized handwriting forms, and speed.

18. Forensic linguistics is the analysis of photographs and sketches as applied to issues of law.

19. Stress caused by deception on the part of a subject can create a graphic disturbance in handwriting.

Multiple-Choice Questions

1. A document that is a forgery is called a(n):
   a. unquestioned document
   b. copied document
   c. questioned document
   d. duplicate document

2. According to the text, when handling paper documents for evidence, the CSI should wear:
   a. latex gloves
   b. cotton gloves
   c. paper gloves
   d. cotton gloves covered with latex gloves

3. According to the text, handwriting or drawings that cannot be physically removed as evidence may be:
   a. duplicated in a sketch
   b. duplicated in the CSI's notes
   c. photographed
   d. traced

4. The organization that publishes recommended standards and procedures for examination of documents is the:
   a. FBI
   b. ASTM
   c. DEA
   d. ICE

5. Spraying a fine mist of _____ and placing charred documents in a box with loosely packed cotton may help prevent further deterioration of the document.
   a. clear varnish
   b. white paint
   c. clear paste
   d. bug repellent

6. The nondestructive lighting technique used to detect chemical erasures on documents is:
   a. infrared (IR) light
   b. ultrared (UR) light
   c. ultraviolet (UV) light
   d. intraviolet (IV) light

7. _____ can be used in examining and differentiating ink on documents.
   a.   infrared (IR) light
   b.   intraviolet (IV) light
   c.   ultraviolet (UV) light
   d.   ultrared (UR) light

8. The type of lighting that helps make latent indentations visible is:
   a.   backlighting
   b.   sidelighting
   c.   frontlighting
   d.   reverse lighting

9. A suspect's natural writing habits are more effectively demonstrated on what kind of documents?
   a.   writing samples provided by suspect
   b.   newly created documents
   c.   normal-course-of-business documents
   d.   older documents

10. According to the text, it is accepted that:
    a.   no two persons have the same handwriting every time but the same person will
    b.   no person has the same handwriting every time nor do two different persons
    c.   individuals occasionally have the same writing every time but not two different persons
    d.   individuals do not have the same handwriting every time but occasionally different persons do

11. Case law has established that the taking of handwriting exemplars for identification purposes:
    a.   is not a violation of the Fourth or Fifth Amendments of the U.S Constitution nor does it require the presence of counsel
    b.   is a violation of the Fourth and Fifth Amendments of the U.S. Constitution and requires the presence of counsel
    c.   is not a violation of the Fourth or Fifth Amendments of the U.S. Constitution but requires the presence of counsel
    d.   is a violation of the Fourth and Fifth Amendments of the U.S. Constitution but does not require the presence of counsel

Discussion Questions

1.   What evidence can be found using documents?

2.   Describe how documents must be collected, stored, and accounted for in order to be used in court.

3.   What characteristics of handwriting analysis can be useful in court proceedings.

12 Motor Vehicles as Crime Scenes

Motor vehicles are an integral part of everyday life—and they are also involved in an increasing number of crimes, ranging from minor traffic offenses to homicides. They can be crime scenes on wheels, and the challenges they pose to CSIs are numerous. Vehicles present the CSI with the necessity of conducting a confined-space search and the need for both interior and exterior evidence collection processes. Not all vehicle searches are performed to collect evidence of criminal activities. Many times the CSI will process a vehicle for the purpose of documenting and collecting physical evidence that may later be used in a civil process to determine fault rather than a criminal proceeding. The protocols and systematic processing remain the same.

Learning Objectives

1. Describe the type of documentation that is imperative when first arriving a crime scene involving a vehicle mishap.
2. Describe the unique photographs that need to be taken involving vehicles.
3. Describe what information can be obtained from skid marks and broken light filaments.
4. Describe the potential evidence when investigating a hit-and-run incident.
5. Explain the most common type of physical evidence associated with hit-and-run incidents.
6. Describe the types of glass that may be found at a hit-and-run incident and how pieces can be helpful during the investigation.

7. Describe the collection techniques that should be used for a hit-and-run investigation.
8. Describe what a chop shop is and what it does.
9. Describe what a VIN is and where it can be found. What information can VINs reveal to the CSI?
10. Explain what product identification numbers and hull identification numbers are.
11. Understand how to process the external surfaces of a vehicle.
12. Understand how to process the internal surfaces of a vehicle.
13. Describe how weather may hinder a vehicle investigation and what can be done to minimize that hindrance.
14. Define "30-day special."
15. Legally, what is the most important issue a CSI must confirm?
16. Explain why using a trained canine dog is preferable if available.
17. Describe how a search of the vehicle should be undertaken.
18. Describe how the CSI should document injuries to the occupant(s).

Key Terms

Chop shop
Driver's point of view
GPS
National Insurance Crime Bureau (NICB)
Point of impact (POI)
Skid marks
VIN

Chapter Outline

I. Documenting the Scene

    A. Photography
        1. Point of view of driver
        2. Measurements of height of driver and passengers
        3. Obstructions
        4. Point of view of potential witnesses
        5. Skid marks
        6. Point of impact
        7. Debris
        8. Light switches
        9. External lights
       10. Seatbelts
       11. Airbag deployment

12. Under hood
13. Tires and undercarriage

II. Hit-and-Run Incidents

    A. Cross-transference of trace evidence

    B. Photograph vehicle

    C. Collect all possible physical evidence from exterior of vehicle

    D. Document pattern evidence

    E. Soil samples

    F. FBI lab(s)
        1. Paint
        2. Glass
        3. Fibers

III. Collection techniques

    A. Paint chips
        1. Packaging
        2. Jigsaw puzzle
        3. Layer structure
        4. Pigments

    B. Glass fragments
        1. At point of breakage
        2. One square inch
        3. Packaging

    C. Check the obvious first
        1. Rear-view mirror
        2. Steering wheel
        3. Gear shift knob/lever
        4. Door handle
        5. Windows
        6. Trunk lid

    D. Weather
        1. Extreme heat or cold will hamper the collection of finger-prints
        2. Move vehicle to a climate-controlled environment if possible
        3. Superglue fuming
        4. Allow vehicle to completely dry before lifting latent prints

IV.   National Insurance Crime Bureau (NCIB)

    A.   Chop shops

    B.   Rip area

    C.   VINs
       1.   Location
       2.   NHTSA requirements
       3.   What the VIN tells us
       4.   Letters I, O, and Q

    D.   Manufacturer's Certificate of Origin (MCO)

    E.   Product Identification Number (PIN)

    F.   Hull Identification Number (HIN)

V.   Stolen Property

    A.   "30-day special"

    B.   Scapegoat cases

VI.   Legal Issues and Searching the Vehicle

    A.   Obtain search warrant if any doubt to the legality of searching vehicle

    B.   Use of a canine

    C.   Dividing the vehicle into search patterns

    D.   Pattern injuries
       1.   Initial photos
       2.   Follow-up photos

True/False Questions

1.   When documenting the scene of an accident or other type of motor vehicle crash, the CSI should take additional photographs compared to other types of crime scenes.

2.   When photographing a motor vehicle crime scene, a 360-degree span should be made at the height of the witnesses.

3.   Skid marks can be used to determine speed and distance.

4.   It is often possible to determine whether breaks in light bulb filaments occurred when the light was off or was activated at the time of the crash.

5. The ATF laboratory maintains reference collections on human and animal hairs.

6. Paint primer layers are often analyzed to assist in the determination of the original vehicle color.

7. The FBI maintains the National Automotive Paint File, which is a database of paints related to all makes, models, and manufacture year of automobiles.

8. Tempered glass is found on all windshields of vehicles.

9. Laminated glass is found on all windshields of vehicles.

10. When possible, paint chips should be collected with disposable forceps and scalpels.

11. When collecting glass fragments for a control sample, a two-inch square is required.

12. At a minimum, the Vehicle Identification Number (VIN) is located on the left (driver) side of the dashboard, the driver side door jamb, and the engine block.

13. Since 1981, the National Highway Traffic Safety Administration (NHTSA) has required a 20-character fixed format for the VIN.

14. The letters I, O, and Q are never used in a VIN.

15. Construction and farm equipment do not have unique identification numbers.

16. Sunlight can cause fingerprints to deteriorate quickly on a vehicle.

17. Forensic scientists are able to determine age from human hair.

18. Forensic scientists are able to determine race from human hair.

19. Scapegoat cases occur when an owner reports a vehicle stolen while hiding the vehicle and then collects a settlement from the insurance company.

20. According to the text, the first step in conducting a search of a vehicle is to ensure that you have the legal right to proceed with the search.

Multiple-Choice Questions

1. According to the text, when documenting the scene of a motor vehicle crash, the CSI must take photographs that accurately depict:
    a.   the point of view of the driver
    b.   the point of view witnesses
    c.   the point of view of passengers
    d.   both a and c

2. When photographing a vehicle crash scene and after determining the correct height of the camera, a tripod should be used to span:
    a.   180 degrees
    b.   270 degrees
    c.   360 degrees
    d.   90 degrees

3. Skid marks made by a vehicle can be used to determine:
    a.   speed and distance
    b.   speed
    c.   distance
    d.   none of the above

4. When two vehicles are involved in a crash, _____ are usually present:
    a.   paint transfer and metal filings
    b.   latent prints and glass fragments
    c.   glass fragments and paint transfer
    d.   glass fragments and fibers

5. The layer of paint that can be used to determine the original color a vehicle is the:
    a.   clear-coat layer
    b.   primer layer
    c.   undercoat layer
    d.   pigment layer

6. The government agency that maintains a database of paints is the:
    a.   ATF
    b.   INS
    c.   DEA
    d.   FBI

7. Evidence that may be created by a vehicle striking a person or object is called:
   a.   pattern evidence
   b.   imprint evidence
   c.   transfer evidence
   d.   impact evidence

8. According to the text, when collecting paint chips or fragments, the CSI should use:
   a.   latex gloves
   b.   latex gloves covered with cotton gloves
   c.   disposable forceps and scalpels
   d.   pocket knife

9. Paint chips and fragments should be secured in:
   a.   brown paper
   b.   a soft container
   c.   paper and a rigid container
   d.   plastic bags and a rigid container

10. According to the text, when collecting a control sample of glass, _____ is sufficient:
   a.   1 square inch
   b. $1^1/_2$ square inch
   c.   2 square inches
   d.   3 square inches

11. The Act that defines a *chop shop* is the:
   a.   Chop Shop Act of 1990
   b.   Anti-Car Theft Act of 1992
   c.   Anti-Theft Act of 1992
   d.   Car Theft Act of 1990

12. Vehicle identification numbers are located:
   a.   left (driver) side of dashboard, transmission, driver-side door jam
   b.   driver-side door jam, engine block, right side of dashboard
   c.   engine block, left side (driver) of dashboard, left door jam
   d.   left-side (driver) door jam, engine block, engine frame

13. The National Highway Traffic Safety Administration (NHTSA) requires a _____ fixed format for all VINs.
   a.   16-character
   b.   17-character
   c.   18-character
   d.   19-character

14. The letters _____, _____, and _____ are never used in VINs:
    a.   Q; O; I
    b.   Z; O; Q
    c.   I; O; U
    d.   Q; U; Z

15. Construction or farm equipment has a unique number called the:
    a.   Hull Identification Number
    b.   Procurement Identification Number
    c.   Product Identification Number
    d.   Off-Road Identification Number

16. Usually a forensic scientist can determine _____ from an adult's human hair.
    a.   gender
    b.   race
    c.   age
    d.   none of the above

17. A _____ takes place when an owner hides a vehicle, reports it stolen, and then accepts a settlement from the insurance company.
    a.   scapegoat case
    b.   60-day special
    c.   90-hour special
    d.   30-day special

Discussion Questions

1.   What unique documentation is required of the vehicle when involved in a crime scene?

2.   Assume you arrive on scene of a known stolen vehicle, and you are preparing to process the vehicle to retrieve any evidence possible to help identify the perpetrator. List what your procedures would be.

3.   What unique documentation is required when motor vehicles come into contact with humans?

# 13 Death Investigation

Death investigation is the most complicated crime scene a CSI will process. Your observations of the victim upon arrival at the scene and the documentation of those observations will play a very important role as the investigation moves through the various stages of completion. Determining how long the victim has been deceased is important in establishing the timeline that will be developed as the final events leading up to the death of the individual are reconstructed.

The protocols followed for conducting the death scene investigation are the same established procedures used for every crime scene. Depending on the complexity of the scene, you may determine that additional resources are necessary, but the steps remain the same. Remember that not all deaths are homicides, but they must be investigated as if they are homicides until the facts indicate that a homicide has not occurred.

Learning Objectives

1. Understand the differences between a coroner, medical examiner, and pathologist and know where to find what system a certain state uses.
2. Describe what an autopsy is, who performs it, and why it is performed.
3. Describe the definition of death in a *medical* sense.
4. Describe the definition of death in a *legal* sense.
5. Describe the five categories for classification of the manner of death.
6. Describe the changes a deceased body goes through.
7. Understand how the medical examiner determines a time of death.
8. Describe the mummification of a body.
9. Describe what adipocere is and why it forms.
10. Describe what a pugilistic position is and how it occurs.
11. Describe what an *epithelial glove* is.

12. Describe what odors a deceased body might have, including when poisoned.
13. Describe what the CSI should document for a death investigation.
14. Describe the different categories of asphyxiation.
15. Describe what causes environmental suffocation.
16. Describe what is meant by *overlay*
17. Understand how carbon dioxide and cyanide cause death.
18. Understand the differences between cut and stab wounds.
19. Describe what is meant by *blunt force, contusion*, *abrasion*, and *laceration*.
20. Describe the indicators the CSI should document at the scene of a sexual homicide.

Key Terms

Adipocere
Algor mortis
Autopsy
Cadaveric spasm
Cause of death
Coroner
Liver mortis
Manner of death
Medical examiner
Mummification
Pathologist
Postmortem interval
Putrefaction
Rigor mortis
Toxicology

Chapter Outline

I.   CSI's Initial On-Scene Actions

    A.   Crime scene protocols the same as conducting any crime scene

    B.   Determine if additional equipment/personnel/experts are needed.
       1.   Arson/fire examiners
       2.   Medical examiner
       3.   Police personnel for security
       4.   Tents or other equipment if outside
       5.   Body clothing—location and position
       6.   Temperature of location of body
       7.   Observation of rigor mortis, liver mortis, and algor mortis
       8.   All injuries before CPR performed

II. Other Investigators

    A. Coroner
        1. Usually no medical background
        2. Usually an elected official

    B. Medical Examiner
        1. Medical background
        2. Usually determines cause of death

    C. Pathologist
        1. Medical background
        2. Assists medical examiner or in some jurisdictions acts as the medical examiner

    D. States' medical and coroner systems listed

III. Autopsy

    A. Detailed external and internal examination of the body of a deceased victim to determine the cause of death, including all toxicology findings

    B. Samples of blood, urine, vitreous fluid, and bile collected

    C. Toxicological samples from gastric organs, muscles, hair, nails, and blood surrounding the brain

    D. Medical examination establishes:
        1. Identification of the deceased
        2. Cause of death
        3. Manner of death
        4. Time of death
        5. Presence of disease or poisons
        6. Nature and number of injuries
        7. Presence of an environmental or health threat to general population

IV. Death by Definition

    A. Medical sense: when a body is no longer performing one of three vital functions
        1. Respiration
        2. Cardiac activity
        3. Central nervous system activity

    B. Legal sense: when all three of the vital functions have irrevocably ceased

C.   Categories for classification of the manner of death
1.   Natural (60%)
2.   Accidental (20%)
3.   Suicide (10%)
4.   Homicide (10%)
5.   Undetermined (1 – 2%)

V.   Post-Death

A.   Rigor mortis

B.   Algor mortis

C.   Liver mortis

D.   Insects

E.   Animal damage

F.   Mummification
1.   Dehydration or desiccation
2.   No future decomposition

G.   Adipocere
1.   Grayish-white waxy/soapy like substance forms on fatty tissues
2.   Damp environment needed
3.   Develops over weeks and is resistant to degradation

H.   Pugilistic position due to fire

I.   Putrefaction

J.   Epithelial glove/boot

K.   Odors
1.   Decomposition/putrefaction
2.   Potential poisons
a.   Cyanide
b.   Fruity, garlic, flowers, mown hay

VI.   Medical examiner case: Any case where a victim suffers a sudden and unexpected death (SUD) and/or that is not attended by medical personnel

A.   Increased scrutiny of individuals who:
1.   Are one to 30 years of age
2.   Are greater than 70 years of age
3.   Have no diagnosed illness
4.   Have no observable injuries

B.   Compilation of information from CSI (notes, sketches, photos) used by the medical examiner to conclude cause of death

VII. Unnatural Deaths

    A.   Poisoning
        1.   Revealed by toxicology tests
        2.   May be gaseous, solid, liquid, vegetable-, animal-, or mineral-based
        3.   May be inhaled, ingested, or absorbed through the skin

    B.   Asphyxiation—three categories
        1.   Strangulation
            a.   Outside pressure placed on neck blocking passage of oxygen
           b.   Hanging and manual strangulation
        2.   Suffocation
            a.   Body no longer has ability to transfer oxygen to cells (21%)
           b.   Smothering, choking, and gases (less than 16%)
           c.   Accidental smothering of child by adult: Overlay
           d.   Choking by food: "café coronaries"
        3.   Chemical
           a.   Carbon dioxide (CD) (normal level +/- 5%) most common
           b.   Cyanide (CN) blocks cellular respiration (almond odor)

VIII. Blunt Force, Contusions, Lacerations, Abrasions

    A.   Blunt force—In order for bleeding to occur, individual must have been alive
        1.   Leaves no visible external injury
        2.   Significant internal damage

    B.   Contusions
        1.   Impact between skin and another object
        2.   Example: hit with stick or falling to ground
        3.   Bleeding beneath skin
        4.   Photograph using 18-percent gray card for reference purposes
        5.   Bruises change over time

    C.   Laceration
        1.   Break in skin
        2.   Edges are irregular and usually caused by the blunt force

    D.   Abrasion
        1.   Surface of skin look "skinned" or abraded and usually created when object comes into contact with skin at an angle
        2.   Deeper form of injury than bruise
        3.   A "pattern" may be visible from the object used to strike victim

IX. Sexual Assault Homicide

    A. Indications of sexual assault/sexual homicide
        1. Evidence of sexual injury or mutilation
        2. Presence of seminal fluid on or near the body
        3. Apparent staging or positioning of the victim
        4. Victim's clothing missing from the body
        5. Presence of substitute sexual devices
        6. Ritualistic or symbolic items
        7. Overkill—numerous wounds inflicted on the victim's body
        8. Bitemarks
        9. Ligatures indicating potential bondage
      10. Pornographic books or videos

    B. CSI must conduct background investigation of victim

True/False Questions

1. Protocols followed for conducting the death scene investigation are the same established procedures used for every crime scene.

2. According to the text, all death investigations should be investigated as if they are homicides until proven otherwise.

3. Generally, a coroner is required to have a medical background.

4. A medical examiner is an elected official and requires little, if any, medical background.

5. Only a licensed physician can determine the manner and cause of death of a person.

6. An autopsy consists of both an external and internal examination of a deceased person.

7. Death occurs in a medical sense when the body is no longer has cardiac activity.

8. In the legal sense, death occurs when there is no central nervous system activity.

9. In 2004, homicide accounted for approximately 20 percent of all reported deaths.

10. At a homicide scene, weapons are rarely found.

11. Lividity or liver mortis is the pooling of blood that causes a dark discoloration.

12. Lividity begins to appear approximately one hour after the time of death.

13. Cherry-red lividity is associated with carbon monoxide or cyanide poisoning victims.

14. The cooling off of a body after death is called algor mortis.

15. The progressive stiffening of the muscles of the body after death is known as rigor mortis.

16. The body is generally in full rigor between 24 and 36 hours after death.

17. After a body has mummified, decomposition continues but at a slower pace.

18. In fire death scenes, it is common to find victims lying in a pugilistic position.

19. Putrefaction begins when death occurs and the body begins to decompose.

20. An epithelial glove refers to the covering that is used for hands before transporting.

21. As decomposition and putrefaction continue, the body becomes brownish is color.

22. Toxicology is the area of science that examines poisons and their effects on the human body.

23. There are generally three categories of asphyxiation: strangulation, suffocation, and chemical asphyxia.

24. The human head and shoulders weigh about 50 pounds; this is enough weight to cause asphyxiation in a standing position.

25. It is impossible to manually strangle oneself to death.

26. Normal room air contains an oxygen content of 71 percent.

27. The accidental smothering of a child by an adult is called overlay.

28. The normal level of carbon dioxide (CO_2) in the air is approximately 5 percent.

29. Cuts are longer than they are deep, and stab wounds are deeper than they are wide.

Multiple-Choice Questions

1. When conducting a death scene investigation:
   a. start from the perimeter to the center of the scene
   b. use the same protocols and procedures as any other crime scene
   c. start from the body outward to the perimeter
   d. use specific procedures for homicides

2. Generally, the official that is required to have a medical background to assist in a death investigation is the:
   a. coroner
   b. CSI
   c. medical examiner
   d. lead detective

3. An autopsy consists of:
   a. a toxicology report
   b. internal and external examinations
   c. both a and b
   d. none of the above

4. Death occurs in a medical sense when the body is no longer performing which vital function?
   a. respiration
   b. cardiac activity
   c. central nervous system activity
   d. all of the above

5. In the legal sense, death occurs when what vital functions have irrevocably ceased?
   a. respiration, cardiac activity, and central nervous system activity
   b. respiration and cardiac activity
   c. cardiac activity and central nervous system activity
   d. central nervous system activity and respiration

6. In 2004, suicide accounted for approximately _____ of all deaths
    a.   10 percent
    b.   15 percent
    c.   20 percent
    d.   17 percent

7. In 2004, homicides accounted for approximately _____ of all deaths.
    a.   10 percent
    b.   15 percent
    c.   20 percent
    d.   17 percent

8. In 2004, _____ accounted for the majority of all deaths.
    a.   homicide
    b.   undetermined death
    c.   natural death
    d.   accidental death

9. After death, the pooling of blood that forms at the lowest portions of the body is called:
    a.   rigor mortis
    b.   liver mortis
    c.   algor mortis
    d.   brown clotting

10. After death, the body begins to cool off. This process is called:
    a.   algor mortis
    b.   lividity mortis
    c.   rigor mortis
    d.   equalization of temperature

11. The progressive stiffening of the muscles of a body after death is called:
    a.   algor mortis
    b.   liver mortis
    c.   rigor mortis
    d.   lividity mortis

12. The amount of time it generally takes for all muscles to have stiffened is:
    a.   12-18 hours
    b.   six-12 hours
    c.   18-24 hours
    d.   24-36 hours

13. Mummification of a body is greatly affected by the:
    a.   temperature of the room
    b.   amount of humidity in the room
    c.   amount of time elapsed since death
    d.   chemicals that caused the death

14. Once a body has mummified:
    a.   decomposition begins
    b.   decomposition increases
    c.   decomposition stops
    d.   dehydration increases

15. In fire death scenes, it is common to find victims lying in a pugilistic position, which is sometimes referred to as a _____.
    a.   defensive stance
    b.   petrified stance
    c.   wrestler's stance
    d.   boxer's stance

16. Skin that has slipped off the hands is known as:
    a.   raw skin
    b.   the epithelial glove
    c.   third-degree burned
    d.   none of the above

17. The human head and shoulders weigh about _____ pounds
    a.   30
    b.   40
    c.   20
    d.   50

18. Normal room air contains an oxygen content of:
    a.   10 percent
    b.   15 percent
    c.   71 percent
    d.   21 percent

19. The accidental smothering of a child by an adult is called:
    a.   underlay
    b.   overlay
    c.   Sudden Infant Death Syndrome (SIDS)
    d.   homicide

20. The normal level of carbon dioxide (CO_2) in the air is approximately:
    a.   2 percent
    b.   3 percent
    c.   5 percent
    d.   8 percent

Discussion Questions

1.   In the medical sense, what is considered death? What is considered death in the legal sense? Discuss the vital functions for each.

2.   Discuss the different categories of death. What is the percentage of occurrence for each?

3.   Discuss the changes a body goes through after death. Howe can these changes assist the investigator in establishing a time and location of death?

4.   Discuss the unique procedure for investigating a sexual assault. Give an example of how time can be crucial in finding evidence.

14 Forensic Anthropology, Odontology, and Entomology

Dr. T. Dale Stewart in *Essentials of Forensic Anthropology* (1979) gives the definition of *forensic anthropology* as "that branch of physical anthropology which, for forensic purposes, deals with the identification of more or less skeletonized remains known to be, or suspected of being human. Beyond the elimination of nonhuman elements, the identification process undertakes to provide opinions regarding sex, age, race, stature, and such other characteristics of each individual involved as may lead to his or her recognition. The CSI should develop working relationships with forensic anthropologists; your paths will cross when you are called to the scene where unidentified remains have been located.

Odontology is the scientific study of teeth and their surrounding tissue. The common name for odontology is dentistry. The forensic analysis of teeth is a separate field from anthropology; however, every forensic anthropologist needs to know the basic knowledge of human dentition, such as the names of each tooth, how to identify an individual tooth, the age when the tooth erupts (comes through the gum), if teeth are deciduous or adult, when they are replaced by adult teeth, and the basic anatomy of a tooth.

Entomology is that branch of science dealing with the study of insects. This section is specific to crime scene investigation, however, and is only provided as an introduction for the CSI into a new sub-area of entomology known as forensic entomology. *Forensic entomology* is the field in which arthropod science and the judicial system interact. The area of forensic entomology has developed in recent years to become an increasingly important aspect of the forensic sciences. Death investigators from every field have observed that in recent deaths, especially outdoors where flies and beetles have easy access, maggots and corpses go together.

Learning Objectives

1. Define *forensic anthropology*.
2. Describe the three areas of forensic anthropology.
3. Describe the two categories of aging.
4. Describe the three best areas from which to estimate age at death.
5. Describe how the sex of a skeleton is determined.
6. Describe how race is determined from the skeleton.
7. Describe how stature is determined from the skeleton.
8. Define odontology. Explain why teeth are one of the best areas of the human skeleton to determine a positive identification.
9. Define *entomology*. Describe how it is used to assist in determining a time of death

Key Terms

Alveolar region
Entomology
Femur
Forensic anthropology
Forensic entomology
Humerus
Mandible
Mastoid process
Maxilla
Occipital bone
Odontology
Sternum
Supra-orbital ridges

Chapter Outline

I. Forensic Anthropology

    A. Dr. T. Dale Stewart: Branch of physical anthropology that deals with identification of skeleton remains of a human being

    B. Usually the last person in the identification chain

    C. Three areas of forensic anthropology
        1. Age at death
        2. Determination of sex
        3. Determination of race

D. Age
    1. Two categories
        a. Maturation
            (1) Dentition—two sets of teeth: deciduous (baby) and adult
            (2) Epiphyses—growth of bones
        b. Degeneration
            (1) Signals end of epiphyses
            (2) Begins in early twenties

E. Age of death of an adult: Pubic symphysis, osteon counting, and osteoarthritic lipping
    1. Pubic symphysis
        a. 1920s—T. Wingate Todd
        b. Compare measurements of unknown specimen with published standards for men and women
    2. Osteon counting
        a. 1965—Ellis R. Kerley
        b. Requires sectioning a long bone (usually the femur) at its midshaft, cutting/grinding/polishing a thin section, and then comparing certain attributes to a published standard
    3. Osteoarthritic lipping
        a. 1979—Steward
        b. Compare stresses in vertebral column with published standard

F. Determination of sex of the skeleton
    1. Pelvis
    2. Skull
    3. Diameter of the head of the femur
    4. Width of articular area of the sacrum
    5. Length of sternum

G. Determination of race of the skeleton
    1. Most reliable area is the skull, specifically the face
    2. 1962—Giles and Elliot published statistical analysis of men/women skulls
    3. Prognathism (most common in negroid skulls)
    4. Nasal sill
    5. Flat face

H. Determination of stature
    1. 2005—William Bass (UT)
    2. Calculations based on the maximum length of the long bones

II. A. Odontology
1. Scientific study of teeth and their surrounding tissue
2. Probably best area of human skeleton to determine a positive identification
3. X-rays
4. Four types of teeth: incisors, canines, premolars, and molars
5. Each tooth has three areas: crown, neck, and root
6. Each tooth consists of: enamel, cementum, dentin, and pulp cavity
7. Each tooth has five surfaces: labial/buccal, lingual, occlusal, mesial, and distal

B. Teeth have unique characteristics such as crowning, misalignment, spacing, staining, and chipping.

III. Entomology

A. Branch of science dealing with study of insects

B. Main focus is to scientifically establish the time of death

C. As a rule, the more time elapses between death and the discovery of the body, the less accurate the estimation of the postmortem interval based on entomological evidence

D. Blow flies are usually the first insect to be attracted to a decaying body

E. Female blow flies lay eggs in moist orifices of body (eye, nose mouth, wounds)

F. Flesh flies do not lay eggs on the corpse but deposit live maggots directly on the natural body openings or wounds

G. The skull, with so many openings, will decay faster than rest of body

True/False Questions

1. The forensic anthropologist is usually the last person in the human identification chain.

2. The areas of forensic anthropology are: determination of sex, age, and race and calculation of stature.

3. Aging can be divided in two major categories: maturation and regeneration.

4. Humans have two sets of teeth: deciduous and adult.

5. Deciduous teeth have usually erupted by 18 months of age.

6. Adult teeth are larger in size and whiter in color compared to the deciduous teeth.

7. There are 206 bones in the adult skeleton.

8. In human identification, the three best areas to estimate age at death of an adult are the pubic symphysis, osteon counting, and osteoarthritic lipping.

9. According to the text, determining age using pubic symphysis is most accurate when the age at death is 70 years or older.

10. Osteon counting uses the microscopic structure of a long bone (usually the femur).

11. Osteoarthritic lipping reflects the various stresses encountered throughout life and the changes in the vertebral column.

12. Men generally have broader hips than woman.

13. The best area to determine the sex of an adult skeleton is from the pelvis.

14. The most reliable area of the skeleton to determine race is from the skull.

15. When determining stature, calculations are based on the maximum length of the long bones.

16. Odontology is the scientific study of teeth and their surrounding tissue.

17. Teeth are probably the least effective area of the human skeleton to determine a positive identification of an unidentified skull with teeth.

18. There are four "types" of teeth in the human dental arch: incisors, canines, pre-molars, and molars.

19. Every tooth has three areas: crown, neck, and root.

20. Entomology is that branch of science dealing with the study of insects.

21. The main focus of forensic entomology is to establish the time since death occurred (postmortem interval).

22. A dead body will decay much faster in the winter than in the summer.

23. As a rule, the more time that elapses between death and the discovery of the body, the more accurate the estimation of the postmortem interval based on entomological evidence.

24. In general the first insects to be attracted to decaying bodies are blow flies and flesh flies.

25. Parts of the body that have openings will decay faster.

Multiple-Choice Questions

1. Forensic anthropology deals with the identification of the _____ of a human.
    a. teeth
    b. skeletonized remains
    c. bone structure
    d. face structure

2. According to the text, the forensic anthropologist is usually the _____ person in the human identification chain.
    a. first
    b. second
    c. last
    d. none of the above

3. The three areas of forensic anthropology are:
    a. sex, race/stature, and age
    b. age, sex, and muscle structure
    c. size of skull, age, and race
    d. bone structure, sex, and age

4. Aging can be divided into two major categories:
    a. regeneration and degeneration
    b. degeneration an adulthood
    c. maturation and degeneration
    d. adulthood and maturation

5. Humans have _____ set(s) of teeth.
    a. one
    b. two
    c. three
    d. four

6. There are _____ deciduous teeth.
   a.   15
   b.   18
   c.   22
   d.   20

7. Usually, by the age of _____, all deciduous teeth have been lost.
   a.   12
   b.   10
   c.   13
   d.   16

8. There are _____ bones in the adult skeleton.
   a.   196
   b.   186
   c.   206
   d.   216

9. According to the text, in human identification, the three best areas to estimate age at death of an adult are:
   a.   pubic symphysis, osteoarthritic lipping, and skull size
   b.   osteon counting, osteoarthritic lipping, and pubic symphysis
   c.   skull size, osteon counting, length of long bones
   d.   none of the above

10. Determining death using osteon counting deals with:
   a.   long bone size
   b.   skull size
   c.   teeth size
   d.   none of the above

11. According to the text, the best area to determine the sex of an adult skeleton is from the:
   a.   face
   b.   skull
   c.   pelvis
   d.   none of the above

12. According to the text, the most reliable area of the skeleton that can be used to determine race is the:
   a.   skull (face)
   b.   teeth
   c.   pelvis
   d.   none of the above

13. Odontology is the scientific study of:
     a. bones
     b. insects
     c. teeth
     d. none of the above

14. The normal number of teeth for an adult is:
     a. 28
     b. 30
     c. 32
     d. 34

15. The branch of science dealing with the study of insects is:
     a. odontology
     b. anthropology
     c. bone structure
     d. entomology

Discussion Questions

1. List what a forensic anthropologist may be able to identify on skeletonized remains of a human. Briefly discuss each.

2. What is the main purpose of forensic entomology? Does the environment contribute to the decay of a body? If so, why?

3. Which insects are typically first to be found postmortem? Do all parts of the body decay evenly? Why or why not?

 # 15 Documenting the Actions of the CSI

CSI personnel are responsible for accurate preparation and prompt submission of all crime scene documentation. The written reports verify the actions of the CSI at the crime scene and must be thoroughly and properly prepared, including copies of all evidence and photography logs. Legible, comprehensive reports must be submitted in a timely manner so that detectives and crime laboratory personnel have access to the information and are up-to-date on all aspects of the investigation. According to the FBI, "physical evidence cannot be over documented."

You should stay abreast of new analytical processes that may impact your profession as well as recent court rulings regarding the admissibility of advancing technologies. Visit the National Law Enforcement and Corrections Technology Center (NLECTC) web site at http://www.nlectc.org to read the latest news about scientific advances. The agency also distributes an electronic newsletter available through the web site for interested practitioners, and maintains a virtual library of resources that can lead you to additional information regarding specific technologies. NLECTC is funded by the National Institute of Justice and provides abstracts of articles, equipment specifications, and grant information to local agencies.

Learning Objectives

1. Understand the importance of proper written documentation.
2. Understand the importance of proper photographs.
3. Describe what the CSI's case file contains.
4. Describe the primary responsibility of the CSI.
5. Describe how the narrative portion of the case file should be written.

6.   Understand who the ultimate audience is for the CSI's report.
7.   Describe what SOPs are and why they should be used by the CSI.
8.   Know what is meant by *rules of evidence* and how they affect the CSI.
9.   Understand the significance of the court case *Daubert v. Merrell Dow Pharmaceuticals Inc.*
10. Know the responsibilities of the CSI, the prosecutor, and the jury or judge.
11. Explain how the CSI should deliver his or her presentation of a case.
12. Explain some of the pitfalls that CSIs may encounter when testifying.

Key Terms

Case file
Case narrative
Comparison samples
Crime scene reconstruction
CSI effect
Equivocal forensic analysis
Known samples
Questioned samples
Standard operational procedures (SOPs)

Chapter Outline

I.   Case Files

   A.   All written reports (case narrative) in chronological order
      1.   Must address the questions: who, what, when, how, and why
      2.   Keep report concise, but include all pertinent information

   B.   All other documentation (photos, tests conducted, etc.)

   C.   Names and other identifying information of all personnel who assisted or conducted part of the investigation (including all forensic assistance)

II. Standing Operating Procedures (SOPs)

   A.   Established by each law enforcement agency

   B.   These are the basic standards that must be followed by the CSI

III. Final Thoughts

   A.   You are trying to present a picture to the jury of the complete case. Speak at a level that the jury can comprehend.

B. Always use other experts, if possible. Too many times CSIs feel they must be the expert in every area of the investigation.

C. Be completely honest. Never make statements concerning the investigation unless it is true and documented in your case file. Remember the rule: If it isn't written in your report, you didn't do it (or it didn't happen).

D. Always put yourself in the jury box. Have someone deliver your testimony while you listen. Would you believe the testimony? Do you have questions, if so, the jurors will probably have similar questions.

E. Never surprise the prosecutor.

True/False Questions

1. According to the FBI, "physical evidence cannot be overdocumented."

2. The "case narrative" is a running description of the entire crime scene investigation.

3. The narrative report must address the questions of who, what, when, where, how, and why.

4. The CSI's primary responsibility is to prove or disprove any theories about the crime.

5. The CSI should offer analysis and/or conclusions in the narrative report to assist the prosecutor of the case.

6. The CSI report should be written in the third person, past tense.

7. The CSI report should not use police slang, radio signals, or jargon in the narrative report.

8. A way for the CSI to ensure proper procedures are being followed is to adhere to the standard operating procedures (SOPs).

9. When labeling evidence, the simple and universal scheme is to label an unknown sample using the letter "K" and the known sample labeled using the letter "Q."

10. The FBI's crime laboratory is located in Quantico, Virginia.

11. Usually, the FBI will process evidence that has already been examined by a state or regional crime laboratory to confirm those findings.

12. The court case that gave the trial judge the responsibility for determining the admissibility of scientific evidence is *Daubert v. Merrell Dow Pharmaceuticals, Inc.*

13. When testifying, the CSI should use technical terms to reflect findings.

14. The agency that maintains the world's largest repository of criminal justice information is the National Repository Center.

15. The organization that maintains the latest news about scientific advances used by law enforcement along with latest court rulings is the National Law Enforcement and Corrections Technology Center (NLECTC).

Multiple-Choice Questions

1. The person who is responsible for accurate preparation and prompt submission of all crime scene documentation is the:
   a. lead detective
   b. forensic scientist
   c. crime scene investigator
   d. prosecutor

2. According to the FBI, physical evidence:
   a. can be overstated, which makes it confusing
   b. should be concise
   c. should offer all potential possibilities to the perpetrator of the crime
   d. cannot be overdocumented

3. The case narrative is a:
   a. running description of the entire crime scene investigation
   b. all the facts and the opinions of the CSI
   c. all the facts and, when possible, the identification of potential perpetrators of the crime
   d. all efforts of the CSI presented in a logical manner

4. According to the text, the CSI's primary responsibility at the crime scene is to:
    a. report all facts that would lead to the perpetrator of the crime
    b. locate, identify, document, collect, and preserve physical evidence
    c. report all facts and opinions that can be used by the prosecutor or defense counsel in court
    d. prove or disprove theories of the crime

5. According to the text, when writing the narrative report, the CSI should:
    a. use the prevailing police terms to ensure exact duplication of terminology used at the time
    b. use terminology normally used by the local law enforcement agency
    c. never use police slang, radio signals, or jargon
    d. use terminology that is common to the prosecutor

6. The written guidelines issued by individual agencies to establish protocols and activities that follow accepted scientific practices is the:
    a. standard procedures for investigations
    b. the CSI's procedure manual
    c. crime scene operating procedures
    d   standard operating procedures

7. _____ are materials or evidentiary samples the source of which is unconfirmed and that are collected at the crime scene and submitted to the crime laboratory for comparison to known samples.
    a. Known samples
    b. Questioned samples
    c. Control samples
    d. Evidence samples

8. Physical evidence from the crime scene that can be compared with samples, victims, and known standards is called a:
    a. comparison sample
    b. known sample
    c. control sample
    d. questioned sample

9. According to the text, the simple marking of physical evidence at the crime scene before sending to the crime lab for analysis is using:
    a. the letter "Q" for known documents and "K" for questioned documents
    b. the letter "C" for control documents and "Q" for questioned documents
    c   the letter "Q" for questioned documents and "K" for known documents
    d. the letter "K" for known documents and "C" for control documents

10. According to the text, a good rule of thumb for the CSI when conducting a crime scene investigation is:
    a. to keep your mind focused on the collection of all possible evidence that the prosecutor can use
    b. to review your actions with "one foot in the courtroom"
    c. to remember that you are trying to prove or disprove all possible theories about the crime
    d. to ensure that all findings, factual or not, are reported in the written report

11. The normal procedure for the FBI's crime laboratory is to:
    a. not process evidence that has been examined by a state crime lab
    b. confirm findings of a state crime lab
    c. provide written analysis of findings but not expert witnesses for court
    d. provide expert witnesses for court but not written findings

12. The court case that gave the trial judge the responsibility for determining the admissibility of scientific evidence is:
    a. *Roe v. Merill-Lynch*
    b. *Furman v. Georgia*
    c. *Moeser v. Mongold*
    d. *Daubert v. Merrell Dow Pharmaceuticals, Inc.*

13. In the courtroom, the CSI should:
    a. express opinions based on the investigation
    b. present testimony accurately and in understandable terminology
    c. present testimony with the intent to be qualified as an expert witness
    d. present testimony as instructed by the prosecutor

Discussion Questions

1. What are the primary responsibilities of the crime scene investigator? What is the importance of written documentation? Who ultimately must be convinced by this documentation?

2. Who determines the admissibility of evidence during a trial? What court case set the standard?

3. Other than becoming a proficient investigator, what other factors must the crime scene investigator possess to be successful in presenting his or her case in a courtroom?

4. Discuss the ethical considerations for the crime scene investigator.